4.50

IN THE HEART
OF THE COUNTRY

IN THE HEART
OF THE COUNTRY

H. E. Bates

Illustrated by C. F. Tunnicliffe

Salem House
Salem, New Hampshire

Published in the United States
by Salem House, 1985. A member of the
Merrimack Publisher's Circle, 47 Pelham Road,
Salem N.H. 03079.

Series design © Robinson Publishing, London

ISBN 0–88162–110–2

Printed in Great Britain

Contents

List of Illustrations

ix

I

Sudden Spring

It is Midsummer Day in the year 1941, the air so quiet and warm in the early morning that you can hear the voice of someone shouting orders to a platoon of soldiers beyond the woods four or five miles away. A little breeze has sprung up in the night. Yellow leaves now and then shake down from the willow-trees, and with them a sprinkle of cotton seed. Savage scarlet stalks of poppy and cool white wands of foxglove are blooming against the apple-trees. The birds are already quiet, but you can hear now and then the greedy, quibbling voice of a young cuckoo, fresh flown from a nest of hedge-sparrows, where he has been fed for a fortnight at the rate of five or six hundred meals a day. For a short time there was the sound also of someone driving wedges into cordwood across the road, but now that has stopped, and the only persistent and continuous sound besides the light sound of wind in summer leaves is the sound of bees working the grey-violet catmint flowers, where the black cat already lies asleep in the sun.

They say it has been the coldest spring for a hundred years, but now the heat is tremendous. The wind began to whip down off the Arctic Circle on New Year's Day, blowing a blizzard of fantastic driftings through the naked hedges wherever there was a high, exposed lie of land, and it blew with ice in it until the second week of June. On June 14th it was so cold that we had hot drinks by a coal fire in the evening of a day that had been as grey as January; on June 15th it was so suddenly warm that all among the yellow water-lilies of the lake the fish were rising and leaping in shoals, and turquoise dragon-flies were quivering mad on the reeds, the water-grasses and the clear, sun-brown water. A day later, in the heat of the evening, a pair of moor-hen went crazy. They began to quarrel first in an island of reeds, flopping and clucking, but at last they came out into open water. Out in the hot sun they did a strange thing. They fought a rearguard action against each other. They spread out their black-and-white tails fanwise like peacocks, and from a short distance made a series of blind, angry rushes at each other backwards, ramming at each other with a stiff fan of tail-feathers. Then for a time they stopped rushing. They began to go round and round each other in circles, sparring for an opening for attack. Sometimes they reversed, then stopped, then began again, movement for movement, until it was like an Apache dance on a floor of lily-leaves. Finally, they made the old tail-fan rush at each other, striking blows with feathers taut and outspread with anger, until eventually something was satisfied and they suddenly ceased and became calm and swam smoothly away. The next day it was so hot that the fish, as you caught them, even under the thick shade of the poplar-trees, died and stiffened in two minutes when you laid them in the grass. Crowds of little steel-blue dragon-flies quivered furiously above the water and among the fawn-gold grass seeds, shaking tiny clouds of pollen from the stalks that were now as high as a man. They poised like blue humming-birds against the scarlet cap of the float, so close that they looked as if attached to it, momentarily like the trembling blue sails of a miniature ship that itself quivered every few moments and sub-merged. Then it rained out of a sky intensely blue and hot without a cloud. The fat, warm drops came down like huge clear bird-droppings, splashing heavily in the water, and the air was no cooler when they ceased. Everywhere there was the heavy fragrance of flowering grass and sun-warmed water and may-blossom, and faintly on the wind the last sweetness of field-beans. The sky had a clear distant splendour, and you had a feeling that summer was everlasting.

A week before it was winter; but now the oats were feathered and the wheat was in ear. The day before the rain came down out of a clear sky I drove to the South from Lincolnshire, where the dykes looked cool on the flat, wide-skied land. Coming down I gave a lift to three Czech soldiers. It was nice weather, I said, and they said: "Yes. Also it is nice now in every country." To them summer, when it came, was a per-manent thing until replaced, at the proper season, by the fall of leaves and finally winter. It was very hot as we drove along, and at last I stopped the car at a hotel and said to the Czechs that we would stop a moment and water the horses. We got out of the car, and the Czechs looked a little bewildered, and I asked them what was the matter. "Please, where are now the horses?" they said.

The English are not a very literal people. Phrases like "Watering the horses" and "It's a nice day" are often just jokes. The English always long for summer, and they know that some time or other it must and will come; but when it does

13

come, they are, as in war, never prepared. They go about in an attitude of astonished and delighted discomfort at the sudden blazing of sun. To them summer-time is an impermanent and ephemeral thing. Earlier in the year, on a cold, raw, May evening bright with sun and golden slopes of cowslips along the railway cuttings, I travelled with a Canadian airman. "I can't get warm," he said. "You never have two days the same." I said : "Yes, but that makes us what we are. The most unprepared people in the world, and yet never surprised." He looked at me and said, "I beg your pardon?" and I could see that he had never thought that perhaps the English had been both hardened and softened, shaped and yet kept plastic, by their extraordinary climate that changes day by day or even hour by hour.

In other countries there is, perhaps, a date for summer, but in England summer, like spring, has no date. No torrents of spring come rushing like thick milk down snow-pied mountain-sides brilliant with tourists and wild narcissi. In towns spring will come, perhaps, at some unspecified date in April, vaguely, with a lovely artificial glory of forsythia-trees and almonds waving in suburban streets, and the townsman is made aware of it, not by something marked on the calendar, but because suddenly, with a slight impulse towards exhilaration, he can walk without his over-coat. But it is very different in the country, where winter is a series of miniature springtimes, a day here, an hour or two there, marked by delicate changes of light, a December catkin on the hazels, a January primrose, a February day bounding with bird-song and calm with flat sunlight drying the overnight rain.

For the third year in succession England has seen a winter of great snows, ice-rain, bitter frost, days of sunless desolation. Yet I remember a day, February 10th, as a day of spring : not the sort of day on which you persuade yourself there is a feeling of spring, a vague air only to be caught at certain moments by sensitive

There was a bright call of bird-song everywhere. Thrushes sang without rest.

persons, but spring in reality. The outside world is taught in its cradle, apparently, one word about the English climate: fog. This word has become irretrievably identified with the obtuseness of English character, so that all over the world the English climate and the English character are cliche's. The climate is foggy, the people are dumb—these are common face-values for England.

But whenever I think of the English weather I think again of two refugees. One was Czech, one German. Both fled their country and came to England. They, too, had been taught, in their cradles, that the word England meant fog. The German had been taught something else: that England also meant in-industry, that in England there was no such thing as the country-side. He had spent his life of forty years with the strange con-ception that England was a series of industrial centres linked by bus-routes. He came to live in Kent, and among the cherry orchards, sweet-chestnut woods, chalk hills, beech-woods and the rich, fertile, flowery sleepiness he had his first lesson about England. The Czech, too, had a surprise. He knew little about England, but he had grown up a very truthful, honest young man. It was only when he wrote home to Prague in the month of February and said, "Here in England the crocuses and daffodils are blooming in the garden and the baby sleeps all day in the sun," that he earned among his people the reputation of being something of a liar.

This February day was just the sort of day which caused the young Czech to write the lyrical truth to his people and not be believed. The sun was strong and warm, and the air was shaken by a light westerly wind; flowers were really blooming in the gardens, and the baby really slept in the sun. The grass was luminous with rain, and from daybreak there was a bright call of bird-song everywhere. Thrushes sang without rest, and even a cock chaffinch lifted a warm claret breast to the sun, trying over and over again the same little trivial notes, pausing, wiping his beak as if to sharpen it on the olive branches of the willow that gleamed with varnished yellow buds, and then tried again. Straws on the hedges, cleaned by snow and rain, were dry and silken again in the sun, bright as daffodils against the plum-dark background of hawthorn. The sallows, like sticks of silver fur, were motionless in the wind, but the hazels moved with the lightest stir of the air, dancing and flagging, leaping horizontally at sudden stronger gusts of wind.

In the garden it was hard to realize that exactly a week before an immense blizzard raged from the north-west, driving through naked hedgerows in vast fantastic drifts of marble dusted a pepper-brown by storms of frozen earth. Now the winter aconites were blooming flat in the sun, a brave lemon-green among tufts of snowdrops. Leafless crocuses, pale mauve touched with fawn, and small alpine anemones, pink and white, were pushing away the drifts of light sepia oak-leaves that have covered them all winter. Here and there a touch of vivid blue, an early grape hyacinth, showed up an eye of magenta-purple, a primula pushing up from wine-veined leaves. The roses on the house wall were breaking with crimson shoots, and the daffodils showed buds low down between twin spears of leaves.

Blessed with one of the most capricious climates in the world, the dumb English have had the sense to import many of the symbols of spring from other people. Not knowing or caring that the grape hyacinth is a weed in every field and vineyard of Southern Europe, the English import it and cherish it, together with crocuses, daffodils, anemones and other imported weeds and treasures, as symbols of the turning year. And as it sometimes happens, as now, that spring breaks a month before its time, the dumb English have the occasional satisfaction of gathering flowers long before people living a thousand miles to the south of them.

17

IN THE HEART OF THE COUNTRY

Even without these imported treasures—and later they can boast wild daffodils, wild snowdrops and even wild tulips ; yes, and wild gladioli of their own—they have two native flowers which by themselves make the early English spring a time of certain loveliness. For countless generations primroses and violets have meant spring to English people.

Between the snows, on sheltered banks, in copses cleared of saplings, both have bloomed all winter. Hazel catkins softened and lengthened in December, were scorched by January frost, and by February were long and sweet again. In times of terrible crisis, when the chance of individual survival is carried about like a frail egg-shell in the hands, are such trivial things worth mentioning? Vague and pompous talk of "new orders," new worlds and new faiths shake the world like the rumblings of an empty belly. Will somebody invade us? Shall we survive? No one, it is said, can foretell what the future holds, what will happen a year from now.

But it is clear that some things are certain and can be foretold. One is the spring. If these islands should one day be invaded by foreign armies, perhaps some young German will know the pleasure, shared by generations of Englishmen, of feeling the February sun warm on his face, of seeing honey-green catkins of hazel and tawny-purple catkins of alder shake in the wind above primroses on the banks of an English stream—and so, like the young Czech, learn his first lesson about England. For climate is more than weather. Climate helps to shape the character of peoples, and certainly of no people more than the English. The uncertainty of their climate has helped to make the English a long-suffering, phlegmatic, patient people rather insensitive to surprise, stoical against storms, slightly incredulous at every appearance of the sun, touched by the lyrical gratitude of someone who expects nothing and suddenly receives more than he dreamed.

II

Fisherman's Luck

You would never guess now that forty or fifty years ago the lake was artificially made. It is hard to think of it now as a great oblong hole scooped out of the mud, fishless, flowerless, treeless, like the pit of a brickworks. It runs now between thick orchards and woods of poplar and hazel and sweet-chestnut on one side, and a lighter fringe of hazel and alder on the other. At the northern end there is a flat meadow with marshy places prickled with sedge. Herons walk about there and flap up at the approach of strangers, and vanish heavily up the river that comes narrowly down between the lake and the trees on the orchard side. There are two islands on the lake, one a mass of willows and reed, the other covered by quince-trees undergrown with ivy and smothered in late spring by big, cool, white flowers and in October by lanterns of lemon fruit. In places wind-massed spears of reed make islands in which duck and moor-hen and coot can get a foothold, and in which occasionally there is a nest of swans. Along the bank odd trees have seeded themselves or have been planted— horse-chestnuts, alders, willows, hazel, elderberries, a wild gooseberry or two. The willows and here and there the alders lean out over the water. It is hard to think of the banks as once being naked, carved out of raw clay. The fringe of reed all along them now is a yard and sometimes two yards wide. Dabchicks hide and dive among them in summer, and voles slide into them and swim out of sight. On heavy days in May colonies of big roach and tench flop among them at spawning-time, and a little earlier you can see cream skeins of perch-spawn tangled among the reedstalks, hatching out to minute fry as the water warms with the sun. Here and there wild irises have pushed even farther out than the reeds, making promontories of clear green and clearer lemon flower in June.

And everywhere there are water-lilies. They are like small yellow water-peonies, and the water all summer seems solid with leaves. In many of the lakes and ponds of the Kentish weald the water-lilies are white, with small claret leaves, and I met a man once who came from a district where the water-lilies were pink. Here they are large-leaved, small-flowered, always yellow. The leaves are so broad that they are stepping-stones for moor-hen and coot, which in summer-time walk from leaf to leaf in a state of dainty bewilderment, heads held sideways, as if puzzled by this strange solidity of water.

It is not until the first warm late May morning, after heavy rain, that the water of the lake begins to have the true green darkness of summer. It lies still in the sun, and the first yellow water-lily buds rigid above it, like golden drumsticks. All over the olive-emerald lily-leaves the rain of the night is caught in drops of quicksilver, and the grasses of the bank are drenched with it. The tobacco-brown tassels of reed flowers are saturated and hang down like over-ripe ears of dark water-corn. The field of beans beyond the lake path is a beautiful moist grey up the slope of land that lies in the sun, and the white and pink flowers, spitted with black, begin to be luminous and fragrant as the heat rises in the blue-white sky.

A month ago the east winds were bitter and dry as they came off the flat water-meadows between the breaks of the trees, and the lake seemed more dead than in the dead winter afternoons when there was no life except a pike or two rising late in the day and a pair of kingfishers patrolling their section of water under the tawny alders. The swans guarding their great reed-basket nest on the bank seemed like snow-birds. The wild duck had paired, the moor-hens lay close among the rising reeds, the water seemed suddenly carved in granite, and, except for a single warm afternoon when the water became alive with a million tiny torpedoes of fish sunning themselves just under the calm surface and a single half-pounder rose to take a cream moth and missed it altogether, there were no fish to be seen. On the dark hedges the stars of blackthorn were very white and frigid, and the drowsy autumn days when the swans rested on the water, their heads under their wings, and fell asleep and let the wind turn them round and round in dreamy waltzing circles, seemed very far away.

Even when the wind turned to south-west and then to south-east and then to south you could still feel the ice in it, and in the evenings the western sky would clear to a pale hard green, and later there would be frost. Then there was a day when the wind blew warm and strong, with a hot sun, and the water cleared to a bright golden-green, and the fish came up in shoals to lie among the shadows of the lily-leaves and rise in hundreds in the calm evening air. You could see even the tench, like chocolate shadows, as they turned slowly in and out of the sunlight. Long, lean pike, sometimes as small as half a pound, lay deadly still in the full sun, snapping suddenly off, heaving up the water like a depth-charge and then becoming calm again. It was hard to see them sometimes, almost yellow in the sun-clear water, hard because they did not move or because when they moved it was too swiftly, but in the deep, clear, leafless pools the roach glided in pink and fawn shoals, and you watched them until they dissolved in the sun, or they suddenly came flipping out of the water, pink and silver, scared by the plunge of a pike. And sometimes the whole depth of water would seem to quiver and become alive as the tiddlers turned in black and silver shoals against the sun.

It was a day that would live in the memory as the first touch of summer. One day it was still winter, and the tips of even the hawthorns were singed with frost; the next you turned and saw the beeches full of a glowing transparence of green, and the bluebells a bright and tender mauve all through the wood that came down to the edge of the water. The white poplars were wonderfully coloured, a bright coppery-yellow, a shade richer even than the oak-flowers, and the horse-chestnuts were in flower on branches that hung far out over the water. The swan brood had hatched; eight cygnets and two parents had made a first excursion up the little river under the darkening alders, and cuckoos were calling everywhere, with the first touch of mid-summer monotony. But it was the blackbirds that caught the miracle of it all, singing clear and mad and warm, in a way that had in it all the heart-break of infinite springtimes.

The urge to fish on a day like this was very great, and you envied the trout and salmon aristocrats, who had been choosing their flies long since with the finicky care of connoisseurs. You remembered the miles of free fishing in Northern Ireland and the stories of your friends who, before the war, took the boat from Fishguard and caught twenty-pounders in the northern lakes. You remembered even the pike you had caught yourself in the middle of winter, and you went over the old lamentations on the spot where the twenty-pound line had broken like dressmaking cotton and the float had careered up and down the lake like a crazy scarlet and emerald buoy all afternoon as the pike fought to get free, until at last it was tangled and lost in a patch of water-weed.

At last the urge was too much. It was still three weeks to the opening of the season. The perch had spawned already along the banks, leaving skeins of creamy jelly woven among the reeds, and soon the reeds would be alive with roach and tench coming in to spawn, too. But there were ponds where seasons did not matter. They were far out in fields by forgotten copses, and were sometimes by abandoned mills and farms, where scarcely anybody ever went. The good ones had carp in them, and most of the others tench and rudd and roach. Most of the fish were little old fish which for some reason never grew to any size, but only, in the case of rudd and roach, to a strange variety of colours, from pure silver down through pink and fawn to a tender gold. Sometimes the tench were big, and if you were lucky there might be rudd up to half a pound. Nobody seemed to know how these old lily-covered ponds had been stocked, and nobody but a boy or two or some chance town-worker on a Sunday bicycle ever went there.

Aristocrat anglers, to whom float and paste are synonyms of heresy, will think it funny how I went to one of these old, abandoned ponds on a warm May afternoon and sat behind clumps of sedge and watched the rudd surface-feeding in the sun. A black windmill with broken sails and a great white and crimson weather-board corn-barn stood on one side of the pond and an apple orchard on the other. The apple-trees were in full blossom, and under the trees a young, good-looking governess was giving afternoon lessons to two girls of fourteen or fifteen. What on earth she was teaching them I don't know, but now and then I caught the word "amphibian" coming across the brown, sunny water, as if, perhaps, the sight of a crazy fisherman fishing out of season had given her a cue. Now and then as I pulled a two-ounce rudd out of the water the girls would look up, and I knew they were not listening. Every time I was ashamed of the fish, but as the afternoon went on and the sun grew warmer and the voices of the girls drowsier under the warm-scented apple-trees, and the light more vivid on the white and crimson corn-barn and the claret lily-leaves, I began to understand something of what fishing is about—why it has remained so deeply in the affections of men, why it has never become an expression of collective social snobbery, why it brings out the best and not the worst of a man's nature. That day I realized that it is not always the size of the fish that matters. All the pleasure there was in the quietness, the sense of communion with place, the feeling of being enfolded, as it were, by the atmosphere that hangs above remote summer waters. The little rudd were quick to snatch the paste off the hook, and were harder to hook than larger fish, and the thrill of catching them after weeks of no fishing was as good as if they had been two-pounders. Towards evening a half-pound rudd came up, and soon afterwards a pair of half-pound tench, smooth and gleaming as copper silk in the evening sun.

About the same time a small boy arrived with a bamboo pole about twelve feet long and a tied line and a jam-jar, and we were pretty well as delighted to see each other as old friends. It was a pleasure to find that there was another fisherman to whom the seasons meant nothing. The boy baited up with breadcrumb

e boy baited up with breadcrumb and began to pull
le rudd out of the pond as easy as picking gooseberries.

and began to pull little rudd out of the pond as easy as picking gooseberries. Every now and then he let out a shout, " Golly, that was a big 'un! He pulled me right under!" but somehow he never landed anything larger than three inches. He talked most of the time he was fishing, and once he said: " Our house got on fire, and our mum and dad and us had to jump out of the window, and the man next door lost nine quid in a chest o' drawers." I asked him his name, and he said: "Mark. I come fishing every night. What's your favourite tune—'The King is Still in London' or 'You'd be Far Better Off in a Home'?" I thought it out a little—the war, the bombing, myself fishing for two-ounce rudd in a lonely pond, out of season, and finally decided that probably I'd be far better off in a home.

I used to go there fairly often after that, always meeting the small boy with the bamboo pole, always wondering if I would, after all, be far better off in a home. The English not only take their pleasures sadly ; conscience also strikes them. It is pleasant nevertheless, and seems quite natural, to see children fishing, and there is something of the small boy in every man who sits by water with a rod in his hand. It seems unnatural to see children on horseback, about to be initiated into the hunting of foxes and deer, but the small boy with his legs dangling on the river-bank has a common charm all over the world.

When the season began at last, the heat gradually increased day by day until it was steady and scorching, with little wind. At nine in the morning—seven by the sun—the heat was sharp in your face and you were already glad of shade. The dew was drying on the grass and the flowers and the dark leaves of the trees. In two days the poppies had burned themselves out, and now, though you did not notice it suddenly, the cuckoo had ceased calling altogether. The hayfields were burning with pink-brown sorrel and pure stars of white dog-daisy and the golden embers of buttercups. The hawthorn bloom was scorched brown by sun, and in the hedges the pink and white dog-roses had taken its place.

By seven in the evening the sun was still clear and fierce, and the water in the lake was as warm as new milk to your hands. The water was very bright, like brown-golden wine, and the fish were not rising greatly and hardly biting at all. They were walking on the water. All evening you could see this happening. Wherever the lily-pads were thick enough you would see great pike coming up at intervals and wallowing in the pads, clear of the water, and then move across the lake, not swimming, apparently, but wallowing on their bellies, playing and moving like seals. Sometimes there would be as many as half a dozen moving at a time, huge brown-steel creatures wallowing in a kind of heavy frenzy of pleasure at the contact of warm air, milky water and sun. Then for a few moments they would lie quiet, and you wondered where they were until suddenly the dark water of a quiet place was splintered with silver scraps of flying fish and the coot were sent screeching into the reeds for cover. Then the pike would play like seals among the lilies again, rocking the leaves like under-water earthquakes, leaving the tall yellow lily-flowers trembling and swaying long after they had gone.

In the heat the fish were not biting well except for a few rudd close under the surface, and at last I changed from bread to caddis grubs. I had never fished with caddis before, and it was like fishing with something that had buried itself alive and then had drowned itself to make sure. The caddis coffin looks like a wooden moth: like a black moth mummified with closed wings. You break away the wings and then you peel away the mummified body. There, buried alive in the wooden case, tight as a finger in a glove, is the caddis, cream-yellow, with a darker bearded head. As a larva it lives its extraordinary coffined existence in water, emerging finally as a fly. Looking it up in the dictionary to find something of its derivation, which appears to be unknown, and still wondering about the small boy and the popular song, and wondering, too, what mad fisherman first broke open the caddis coffin to find a new bait, I came across what was for me a new expression. For it seems that in French a strait-jacket is a " camisole de force "—which is exactly what the caddis lives in.

I caught a perch with the first caddis, getting a sudden furious bite and a steep dive, as if the fish, too, were mad. He was lively but not large, and I gave him to a soldier fishing farther up water with a sea-line, breaking-strain about fifty-six pounds, no rod and a couple of wine corks. He fixed the perch for live bait, and very soon had a four-pound pike which he hauled in like a battleship's anchor. They are fishing every evening, the soldiers. Some have been fishermen and have sent home for tackle. Some have never angled. They come with sea-lines but no floats and lay half an Army loaf on the bottom. They come with broomsticks, lengths of packing-string and bent safety-pins. They come with the indomitable hope and crazy enthusiasm of all fishermen, and fishing is saving their lives.

Seeing them so often without floats, I thought of making and distributing some. For floats of light and sensitive balance are easily made from crows' quills. So I sent the children searching for feathers, hoping for a dozen, but they had the sense to search under the trees at the rookery and came back with a hundred and twenty-five. We painted them bright red and green or left the natural coffee-black shade untouched, which is probably better.

Fishing, I think of Uncle Rook. He is the piscatorial saint of the family, a nineteenth-century local Walton on my father's side. Few obscure local idlers remain a legend forty or fifty years after their heyday. But this is true of Uncle Rook, who never worked but could angle like an angel. For I remember a year ago going home to the Midlands and one morning taking rod and line to sit by the bank below the old, decayed wharf with the now-derelict pub, where boats and beer were the great summer pleasures forty or fifty years ago. There were four or five men fishing, two at least of whom I knew, and one solitary figure bent on the bridge. We fished for a little while, but it was very dull, and we began talking. I forget how it came about, but someone called me by name, and soon the men knew who I was, that I was kin to Rook, still a legend on the river, and I remember there was quite a silence of admiration. We sat there talking of this angel of fishermen for some time until at last we looked up to see the solitary figure coming wearily down from the bridge.

"Any luck?" we said. "Had a touch?"

"Touch o' bloody agony."

He sat down on the bank and threw in his line. It was one of those dead sad mornings when instinctively you feel that fish are lifeless and when in the end there is nothing to do but talk. I should have set down the conversation at the time, because it was a remarkable conversation for four factory hands, a lorry-driver and one writer to be making on a drowsy English Sunday morning during war. I know that it ranged from America to Hitlerism, from the best baits for roach to the philosophy behind James Hilton's "Lost Horizon." "A roach," said the man who had come from the bridge, "'ll tek anything when it's a-mind. I never had no luck one Sunday until I got damn well fed up and put a lump o' baaked pudden on. I had a pound roach straight off. Ah, true as I sit here. Yis," he said, "and I caught another wi' a lump o' cold sausage. Put the bloody sausage on and down she went."

He talked for a long time in the broad, droll accent that

extends all down these eastern river valleys—the Ouse, the Nen and the Welland, out beyond the Fens and the siltlands, probably as far as the sea. That language is naturally humorous, descriptive, pungent. It has been called a language that "has filled a remarkable destiny." It has been said that "the English of books and modern speech is not the tongue of Northumberland ; it is not the tongue of Wessex ; it is the tongue of these eastern shires of Mercia which border on East Anglia," and, again, that "there can be no doubt that the English language, in the form that has been classical ever since the fourteenth century, is the language of the shires bordering on the great monastic region of the Fenland, the tongue of Northamptonshire, Huntingdonshire, Rutland and Holland. . . . Classical English is neither northern nor southern, but midland ; and of midland it is eastern and not western. Anyone may convince himself of this who has learned enough of the dialects of England to know how much nearer the tongue of a Northamptonshire peasant comes to the English of books than the tongue of a peasant either of Yorkshire or of Somerset."

So this fisherman, talking of baiting for roach with "pudden" and sausage on a September Sunday morning, was talking a language nearer to both classical and common English than he could possibly know. Everything he said had a natural pungency, decorative yet unforced, and I remember we forgot to fish because we laughed so much. I discovered afterwards that he was much impressed by my presence : for two reasons. First, that I was kin to the classical Rook, whom he had doubtless known at the height of his skill on that river ; and, second, because "I bloody well knew he was a gentleman, an' all. I could tell by the way he spoke." If only he could have known how much more a gentleman I thought him, and how impressive and attractive to me his own speech was, the speech that seems

30

to have in it the same broad, direct flow and flavour as the waters of the rivers by which it is still spoken.

Back by the shores of the lake, or under the alders by the narrow river where the summer water is creamy-brown and weedless and almost without flow, I wonder continually what it is that attracts men to fish, and, having once attracted them, keeps them mesmerized for life. For there is something mesmeric about it. You can sit sometimes by water when the wind is rippling it into small rapid waves and watch the float until the waves and the scarlet cap produce a queer feeling of magnetism, so that you are no longer certain whether the waves are moving forward under the wind or the float backwards under the pull of a fish. You hear people say that fishing is a waste of time. Can time be wasted? Whatever time theory you have, your life is, or appears to be, a progression in which birth, eating, sleeping, walking and death are major and continuous elements. In a hundred years it will not matter much whether on a June day in 1941 I fished for perch or devoted the same time to acquiring greater learning by studying the works of Aristotle, of which, anyway, I have no copy. The day is very hot, and there are thousands of golden-cream roses blooming on the house wall in the sun. Perhaps someone will be glad that I described them, sitting as I am forty miles from the German lines at Calais. Perhaps someone will wonder then at the stoicism, the indifference, the laziness or the sheer lack of conscience of someone who thought roses and fish of at least as much importance as tanks and bombs.

III

Overture to Summer

Meadow-sweet is beginning to bloom by the waterside, and the air is heavy with the dusky odours of high summer. The grasses are as tall as a man. It is ten years within a week or so since we came to live in Kent. The grasses were as tall as a man then in the meadow that is now the garden, the docks were like parsnips, and I remember that the autumn was so tender that the meadow-sweet went on blooming until November and no one could plant fruit-trees and rose-trees because there were no frosts to bring down the leaves. The shrubs we planted then have grown far beyond what I suppose we ever hoped they would. A little cutting of a Cupressus plumosus, given us in a pot, is now nine feet high; another of a Japanese juniper, of a prostrate habit, is now four or five feet across. On the other hand, the little columnar Irish junipers have hardly grown at all, and the tiny trees of Rosa Rouletti, like minute pink ramblers only six inches high, have hardly put on a centimetre.

The children yesterday were asking how long plants live. If there were plants which live for ever? Some of the delphiniums we planted ten years ago are still as vigorous as ever. A red tobacco plant, against all rules, comes up year after year under the shelter of the house wall, but whether from seed or from the same root I can never tell. I imagine vigorous things like Oriental poppies, Michaelmas daisies, heleniums, even madonna lilies, will live easily for forty or fifty years. Roses, especially climbing roses, will live at least the lifetime of a man, and, I should think, even longer—perhaps a hundred years. There must be trees of Gloire de Dijon that were planted as novelties when the rose was introduced in the nineteenth century that are still growing today. Is there a rose of equal quality? It always seems to me not so much a flower as the emblem of a period: like a creamy elegant bosom slightly flushed.

The house-sparrows have nested again under the eave where the Gloire de Dijon climbs up the house, always flowering twice a year, and now as I sit here the old birds are feeding the young. They come down to the lawn in front of me, and the young sit in a state of quivering excitement, squeaking a little, while the old birds forage among the grass for food. And, as they feed the young, others are gathering, even as late as this, material for still another nest. The sparrows are very tame and come often to sit on the table as I write. A hen chaffinch became even tamer once and used to perch on chairs and tables as we ate meals in the garden in summer, and for a time there was a brown mouse who used to come round the corner of the summer-house and search for fallen crumbs and then suddenly fall over himself in his haste to get away.

IN THE HEART OF THE COUNTRY

But this year all the joy of spring has been in the singing of blackbirds. Are blackbirds individualists? You hear a wren singing the same sweet little run of grace notes over and over again. A yellow-hammer on hot midsummer afternoons beats at the drowsy silence with the same monotonously beautiful bar of song, but it seems to me that blackbirds are inventive, that there is no such thing as a blackbird's song common to all blackbirds, but a whole range of invented melodies that vary according to the individual environment of the bird. In a group of sweet-chestnut trees near the house there is a blackbird that has sung all spring, through both warm and bitter weather, with a peculiar honey-madness, as if he were out to break your heart. His range is great, but the quality of his singing has individual style, so that to hear him is not just to hear a blackbird, but a Mozart among blackbirds, a creature singing with rare flavour and recognizable charm of character. But there is another, by the lake, who sings quite differently. He is just a street comic, the errand-boy whistling with the basket. No poetic passion, no breaking the heart-strings. He whistles like a boy whistling a girl in the street—whew-oo-whit! You listen, and then he calls, as clear as if he had picked it up like a parrot from a fish-seller somewhere on the coast: "Fine whiting, fresh whiting!" Somehow he has got hold of these notes, which to us are recognizably human, and made them his own and kept them. We know, as James Fisher has pointed out, that birds don't have ideas, that the idea of the male bird sitting and singing on the bough to charm the loneliness of the sitting female is just a fanciful human idea, not a conscious consolatory gesture of the bird's. But this singing of the blackbird's seems, at any rate, like an idea. The song of the blackbird by the lake is fixed: six notes. It remains fixed, never varying, except that sometimes the sixth note is dropped, and is repeated scores of times a day, bell-clear, hundreds of times a week, comic and mocking over the beanfields and the water. So that even if half a score of blackbirds were singing there you could pick out this one comic, with his charm-you-to-death fish-call, from all the others. This seems like a manifestation of individuality, and it is tempting to be sentimental about it and call it conscious artistry. It can't be, of course, but as evidence of the blackbird's power to produce variations of notes and then make these notes individual by repetition it is remarkably interesting and, even taken as a mere triumph of instinct, a wonderful thing.

"We do things to birds," says James Fisher, "and they do things to us." Behind that simple statement there lies all the fascinating age-old history of birds and man, a history largely unwritten but now being very capably written by men like Fisher, for whom birds are not merely an æsthetic decoration to man's existence, pretty creatures with, so to speak, man-reflected ideas like that of singing to cheer their lonely mates, but for whom the attraction of birds lies, among other things, "in the web of behaviour-patterns which makes up the system of the bird's life" and in the history of "nesting and courtship and oology and migration and speed and weight and food and protection" of which every species provides a bewildering quantity of material.

We know that birds are adapted in many ways to their environment, but I am puzzled as to why on this rich valley land there are few larks, so few that a burst of lark-song is a rarity, and why, incidentally, there are few hares. Clay-land is rich in larks, and it is also on clay-land, especially some of the clay-land of Hampshire, that you will find hares so common that it is nothing to see forty or fifty or even more feeding and galloping in a field. By association lark-song ties me to the clay-land of my boyhood, and as I hear it in memory I see legions of April cloud-shadows rolling and racing over valley-sides of young corn, and I feel the cold spring rain on my face and the harsh, rocky clots of clay turning my ankles as I walk across the furrows. But here, off the clay-land, I neither hear larks nor see hares, and it was a pleasure on a March day this year to go down to the flat clay-land of the Weald and there, on a drizzling-light afternoon after heavy rain, hear larks singing in choirs above a land that was a desolate yellow with water.

There are always larks, too, on downland. On some breezy warm June afternoon we go up to the slopes below the chalk-scars and the beech-woods that top the hills, to find the wild straw-berries ripe. After living in the valley, where horizons are cut short by trees, it is a shock of delight to find the world so broad.

Yesterday as we climbed the hills there was a light north wind, fresh but not cool, blowing against the heat of the sun. The clouds were white, like slow-moving airships as they came over the hill, but under the shelter of beech-woods, on the open slope of down, it was very hot, and the wild strawberries were ripe everywhere. They grew among the fallen larch-twigs, under brambles, partially hidden by clumps of bryony, on the chalk paths, under bushes of wild rose and elderberry, between patches of wild mignonette and pink orchis and wild valerian. You could gather them, not by ones or twos, but by the basketful, and as you stood up straight from gathering them the world of broad, sun-drenched down and valley and blue-white sky suddenly tipped and revolved as if top-heavy with the rich weight of summer. The larks were suddenly shrill in the afternoon silence, broken otherwise by nothing but the ceaseless whirr of grasshoppers and the wind creaking the beech-boughs, and now and then by a bomber or two coming home from France. If you wanted to know what it was like to live in England in the year 1841 or even 1741, all you had to do was to stand there and look down at the great green landscape below. It was, perhaps, a little different;

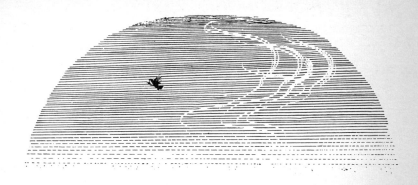

*I lay down and went to sleep
with the sun on my face.*

perhaps there were more hedgerows or fewer trees; but all you had to do really was to cut out the concrete water-tower from the middle distance, the home-coming bombers and the masts of the radio station just visible like grey needles above the far coastline. You cut them out and you had left a landscape of trees and little church-towers and grass and corn rising into green ear. It looked eternal, and you knew that if you had nothing else in common with an English peasant of the hungry forties or a country parson of the seventeen-forties, you had this view. You were looking at the same hills and perhaps at the same shape and colouring of fields; you were, perhaps, looking at many of the same trees, most likely the beech-trees and the giant sycamores that shaded the eighteenth-century house in the village below, and you were certainly looking at the same churches. And except for the bombers you were hearing the same sounds: larks singing, the north breeze in the thick beech-boughs, an occasional cock-crow from the farms below the hill, the hot whirr of grasshoppers.

We went on gathering strawberries until at last, for me, the world went round once too dizzily. I lay down and went to sleep with the sun on my face. Waking up, I did not know which day it was or where I was, and my face was oily with sweat. I might just as easily have woken to wonder what year it was or if Napoleon had landed at last on the flat sands of Rye and Camber. A few more people had come to gather strawberries, and one of my children was running to catch a butterfly. "I sawed him and I runned after him. But just as I got there he put his brakes off and went away."

There was, perhaps, just one other thing you could see from this hill-top that could not have been seen a hundred or two hundred years ago. Where the chalk breaks out below the woods the slope in one place spread out a pale delicate blue: a field of flax in flower. It had a kind of trembling wateriness in

38

the heat, as if the normally barren, sun-scorched slopes were being softly flooded. In the same way flax has been changing the southern countryside throughout the spring. Huge lorry-loads of it brush through the narrow lanes on their way from farm to factory, and then later from farm to field. For in early spring the flax-crop is laid out in swathes in meadows, like a dream hay-crop that has never been picked up. It is laid out, not to dry, as might be supposed, but so that the process of rotting, or retting, can be hastened. It lies on the grass throughout April and early May, and sometimes there is the warm, sweet odour of it on the air. In mid-May it changes from a hay-crop to a Lilliputian corn-crop, bound into little sheaves and set up into little shocks. It is now darker brown in colour, the shade of old house-thatch, and where the swathes have lain the wood-pigeons come down to feed on the fallen seed. And now, if you pick up the stalks, you can see what flax is and what this spring rotting has done. As you pick it up now it disintegrates into fine silver fibres, delicate but tough, that have already some of the sheen of linen.

By mid-June the flax has been picked up and the fields are clean again. After rain the moon-daisies are tall and the sorrel is lush, pink-brown, waving in the sun. If the beauty of the English countryside depends largely on the design given to it by good husbandry, how much does its more intimate beauty depend on the things which even good husbandry cannot dominate or destroy—for instance, weeds? Kex in flower is like green lace in all the May hedgerows, and sorrel in flower makes waving crests of bronzy-pink feathers in late June. The beanfields, green now with young pods, are spitted with scarlet drops of poppies as regularly as if they had been painted by machine. A month ago there were fields of buttercups far brighter than mustard or charlock, as if yellow paint had been poured across them in a river. And everywhere now the moon-

39

daisies are crowded in grass, pure and shining as the high noons of midsummer and the long amber-clear twilights.

Some day someone may write a book on weeds, showing their place in the natural scheme, showing how the weeds of one country—Switzerland or Tibet or Peru—are the show-flowers of another. There are weeds which are very lovable. The scarlet pimpernel of cornfields, more russet-orange than scarlet, is an affectionate thing; so is the small cream wild pansy that grows with it. There are weeds that are aristocrats: sailor-blue vipers' bugloss, butterwort, white campion; but as soon as you begin to name them you cross the line between weeds which are weeds and weeds which are wild flowers, and you become entangled in the glory of primrose and bluebell and wild iris and wild Canterbury bell and meadow-sweet. You get caught up in the train of weeds that are crops—white and pink clover—and the weeds which, like the New Forest gladioli, are rarer than garden flowers. But some day someone will write that history. Someone will show the part played by weeds in the lives of animals and birds, and so in the life of man, and how, both economically and æsthetically, life would be poorer, perhaps even dislocated, without them.

IV

Fruit Blossom Time

Our part of the village is called the Forstal : literally, I think, forestall, the settlement occupied before the village proper ; a village green. Anyway, like most Kentish forstals, it stands away from the main body of houses, which in turn, in our case, stands away from the church itself, so that we have a tiny hamlet split into three even smaller hamlets, the extreme ends about two miles away from each other. The Forstal stands high and is an egg-shaped green of grass surrounded by a ring of warm, red-brown houses on one side, a group of stone houses on the other, and on the north side what is called a platt of trees. And at the western end lies the pond, deep and dark behind overhanging chestnuts and willows and bushes, and freshened by yellow water-lilies by the southern edge. From this combination of trees and water and open grass and old houses there arises a very pleasant sense of harmonized security.

Over a period of years the pond has become the centre-point of the green. By itself water can be very attractive, but once there are birds on it and fish in it the attraction is greatly multiplied. Ten years ago the pond had swans on it. They were fed daily by a pleasant old gentleman. But the swans died and then the old gentleman died and the pond for a time became, as we thought, lifeless. In cold winters we skated on it, a thing which no cautious inhabitant had ever dared do before, and sometimes on red crackling January afternoons the ring of ice was like a white dance-floor full of laughing children. In very hot summers the water became greasy and dead, with a surface scum of green-brown slime. Then we began to keep ducks, the fawn-brown Khaki Campbell kind, which departed from the house in the morning and came back to the house for tea in the evening. At once the ducks gave back to the water, besides keeping it clean, some of the visual attraction it had had in the days of the swans. Now when people passed by they would stop to look : to watch the ducks standing on their heads, the drakes flying and splashing crazily, or the whole brown flotilla lining up in order as they were called home for food.

Then something else happened. The eldest of the children, aged eight, went off to the pond one evening with a rod and a tied line, baited the hook with far too large a piece of bread-paste, and in three minutes hauled in a pair of weighty tench. Since no one had ever known the pond contained tench or any other fish, this was an exciting moment. As if to prove that it was no fluke, she repeated the performance the next evening, again with two tench, and again the following morning, but this time with four tench and a handsome rudd with a belly like a sow. The next morning it was repeated again, with a rather smaller rudd and five tench, all of decent size. Since the process was the simple one of laying a lump of paste on the bottom and getting a bite almost before it had reached the bottom, it appeared likely that the pond was crowded with tench which had been there for years. So the pond at last conformed with the tradition of the Wealden ponds, which are full of ancient tench and sometimes rudd that may, by some accounts, have been put there in the eighteenth century. How tench came to be in the pond here, and to grow to tolerable size, without the fact ever being noticed or exploited, no one knows.

By this time the banks of the pond were lined with every small boy in the neighbourhood impatiently swinging out lengths of packing-string and farthing hooks hung from garden canes, and all anxious to improve on the performance of a little girl. But so far not one tench has come out of the pond on any rod but hers, and she remains the triumphant local female Walton, a very true descendant in the third generation of Uncle Rook, who, too, had the reputation of being able to take fish with ease where other men sat for hours without a nibble.

They say that tench begin to bite when the corn is in ear, and on this first day of July the corn is in ear. It stands straight and dark, the ears pointing rigidly upward. Clover and hay are being mown now in the most forward meadows, and gradually you can feel the tune of summer deepening to full harmony. There is no better month than July, when haytime and harvest are fused and peas are in pod and the potato-fields begin to flower mauve and white and the dominant light everywhere, on corn and grass and flowers and even by water, is yellow, the full-coloured distillation of sun.

The orchards, too, are coming into their second period of glory. The cherries are ripening; the tall ladders are set among

43

the dark, cream-pink sprinkled trees, the round baskets stand piled in corners. There is heavy shadow under the enormous canopies of cherry-leaves, so much thicker than plum or apple or pear, and it is difficult to remember the early spring days of naked branches and even the later days when every bough was luminous as snow with flower and scattered petals covered the grass and scattered sunlight the showered petals. The orchards begin to move into life as far back as February, sometimes in January, in warm winters in December : not cherries or plums or apples, but orchards of hazel, which hang out avenues of slanting, honey-green catkins that seem smokily luminous in the flat winter sun.

In the whole English fruit year there is nothing quite like this first soft wintry blossoming of millions of catkins, when countless flowers swing away from the wind together and stand out horizontally in air, poised in golden parallel, almost flying, then falling away and dancing in the moments of dead calm.

The avenues are so straight and formal and the pruning of the trees so rigid that the catkins seem like irresponsible things, too frisky and delicate for squat trees pruned of their grace. And I imagine hardly anyone ever sees these first nut orchards blooming in mid-winter ; and I imagine, too, that for every hundred persons who see them only one, perhaps, sees their millions of other flowers : the almost invisible firmament of minute female flowers, like ragged scarlet stars, that hide behind the dancing curtains of the males.

Between these early orchards and the real bonfires of blossom there is a gap of a month or more. In the old orchards of the South it is partly filled—you might almost say illuminated—by snowdrops. They suddenly cover the old winter grass every-where, white crops of petals, like flakes, drifting thickly sometimes among the sheep-pens, where first lambs hobble from behind the wind-breaks of yellow straw. And towards the end of March,

...erry blossom comes in royally
...heavy clustered sheaves.

or early in April, geese will replace the whiteness of both lambs and snowdrops. They seem to like orchards, and come back year after year to build their nest in the same place, guarded with fierce and rather comic devotion, under the budding trees.

I am writing of the South, where in many districts plums and cherries predominate over apples, and where few pears, except the delicious long green Conference, are grown, and it would be hard to say which blooms first, cherry or plum. I think perhaps the earliest plums break first, creamy-headed and never really white even when open, but always touched a little with green and cream. The April distances still being sombre, the plum orchards are almost always a misty surprise when seen from afar off, half melting into the breaks of the land, entirely melting into a sky of broken cloud. They will be seen at their best from hill-tops or against hill-sides, and at their very richest when the Victorias bloom, with their larger blossoms of pure dazzling whiteness, against which all other plums seem like faded ivory.

But if the plum orchards have a certain laciness, so much part of the sketchy April scene of half-colours and quickly changing light, the cherry orchards have a rich and glorious solidity. They seem like a festival. Plum bloom is sprinkled along the bough, but cherry bloom comes in royally in heavy clustered sheaves, bountifully, and yet, because of the long flower-stalk, with grace and lightness; the trees are bigger, sometimes vast, the bloom bursts in great festoons from every bough, and the whole blossoming is like a harvest of flower. There is nothing—in England, at any rate—like the flowering of the cherry orchards in the first days of May, so prodigious and magnificent that the white branches are sometimes weighed down, as if by fruit, on the extreme orchard edge, where sun ripens the fruiting wood and in July brings the white-hearts swinging down to the dog-roses in the hedge-side.

46

No one who has ever seen that prodigious snowiness of the cherry orchards will doubt that cherry-land has sometimes ten times the value of the best farmland, and that one good season of cherries is said to compensate handsomely for two that are bad. And it is strange that with the fruit colouring so differently— pink, cream, scarlet, black—there is no corresponding variation of flower colour. Even the little black Morellas, flowering and fruiting rather late and less heavily than the ordinary kinds, have still that pure, constant whiteness.

It is the apples that break the rule of whiteness, by which pears are also governed, though the fat pear-blossom buds are some- times almost golden, with the honey touch of pears themselves. But there are few pear orchards and, unhappily in England, no peach orchards. In the apple orchards alone is there a break into colour. Shades of pink deepen and pale all through the range of apple varieties : the silver-pink of shells ; the cool pink of wild roses ; the true, clear, wild, crab-pink ; the deep vermilion-pink of some large late-flowered variety like Lord Derby.

And so the apples, coming last, are to my mind—in spite of Housman—the loveliest of trees. The blossoming of apples is warmer, more summery ; it is an individual as well as a collective thing. The cherry has in it a touch of northern snowy beauty ; its loveliness comes entirely from the white wonder of the great shining masses of flower. But each apple flower has individuality : a button-hole flower, friendly ; that you feel you must break off and cherish and smell. For there is no sweetness like the clear, affectionate fragrance of apple bloom, pure and delicate and joyous, blown in over the edge of summer.

And apple orchards, low and level in the valleys, rising pink on the hill-sides, can also be seen. The eye, in late April, no longer searches the bare distances, uncertain whether it sees blossom or smoke. The backgrounds have come : beeches and

47

chestnuts leafing, oaks in flower, the hedges like walls of emerald. And against them, and above the orchard grass that is suddenly alive, too, with buttercups and twittering yellow chickens and the gosling comedians that roam in line among the fallen petals, the pink orchards stand out like new paint, warm, bright, tran- scendant, part of the new and only cloud-cuckoo-land.

V

"*Clouded August Thorn*"

*T*he names of flowers become sprinkled into the language, meaning changed, as symbols, as labels of affection or contempt, as synonyms of types of character. It's a daisy, we say; he's a pansy. Somebody wears the white flower of a blameless life; is as pure as a lily; is the Scarlet Pimpernel. Fruit has a still more remarkable influence. You play gooseberry; you give a raspberry; a girl is a peach, a job is a plum, a child the apple of his mother's eye; a bomb is a pineapple, you're not worth a hatful of crabs, and the answer's a lemon. But except for the word "butterfly" itself, nothing of the names of moths and butterflies, except the Camberwell Beauty, seems to have penetrated into the common speech. Yet the names of butterflies and moths have some of that same delicious fancy that makes pub-names one of the most fanciful things in English life. Are these, for example, the names of wayside inns? The Spotted Elephant, The Black Arches, The Ground Lackey, The Glory of Kent, The Green Forester, The Lulworth Skipper, The White Admiral, The Purple Shades, The Brixton Beauty, The Rosy Rustic, The Beautiful Pug, and The Dover Belle. No, they are the names of moths and butterflies. Similarly, these are not the titles of books, though they might well be : The Crimson Speckled Footman, The Light-Feathered Rustic, The Black Chestnut, The Cambridge Veneer (I commend this to a social satirist), The November Dagger, The Belted Beauty, The Essex Emerald, The

49

IN THE HEART OF THE COUNTRY

Long-Legged Pearl and The Ringed China Mark (two beautiful titles which might fit anything from detection to poetic fantasy), The Beautiful Snout, and, lastly, what I shall choose as the title of this chapter, The Clouded August Thorn.

These four words, it seems to me, have some of the quality of August in them. Once I remember hearing a man say: "I hate August." It is hard to know what prompted him. He had, he said, an impression of aridity, of everything being dried up, that was dull and tiring. From this I gathered that his feeling for the country was obtuse. There are no dull months in the country, no single month that is continuously hateful. And it is a simple fact that August is the richest month of the year, perhaps the most beautiful of all months, the great period of fruition when it is only necessary to hold out your hands to have them filled with harvest. It is a month whose rich, dewy fruitfulness seemed to be in the name of that sun-brown butterfly, the Clouded August Thorn.

The fortieth August of this century was more memorable and more exciting than any August in England has perhaps ever been. There has never been, and perhaps never will be again, an August of its kind. All summer in the South the planes coming in from the coast had been gradually increasing in number, from the morning when we woke up and went out into the garden and smelled in the already warm, calm air the smell of burning oil being borne inland on the south-east wind from Dunkirk, to the August Sunday noon when the first black bomber came crashing down in the hot sunshine and I wondered what it felt like to be dying on that very peaceful morning a mile or so above the early ripening corn of a strange country. As more planes began to fall and more parachutes began to flower in the sky that had been an almost unbroken blue since the middle of April, the nerves of everyone became very hard and strained, like catgut pulled out to

The August Sunday noon when the first black bomber came crashing down in the hot sunshine.

its limit and left stretched and dry. My own nerves were no different from those of anyone else, and underneath what I hoped was a fairly calm and even indifferent exterior I felt myself growing very near to a breaking-point, not necessarily a breaking-point of courage, but probably a breaking-point of faith, beyond which the beauty of the August countryside, the joy of living in it, the purpose of harvest, and even the tangible results of harvest would become a mockery that had only an automatic meaning.

At this moment we were paid a visit by my brother-in-law, who is a Nene Valley man and therefore almost automatically an angler. At this time I did not know the difference between a roach and a perch—at least, not very clearly—and the total weight of my life's fish was probably about six ounces, which included some gudgeon taken by the simple process of dangling a worm in front of their eyes and hoping for a positive result. Though I came of a family of fishermen, from a fishing district, the fishing instinct in me was merely latent, and it might have remained unroused except for the attempted invasion by air by those hordes of silvery fighter planes whirling like seagulls above flocks of bombers flying like black geese over the ripening Kent countryside.

So at a suggestion of mine, made primarily as a gesture towards a relative who was also a guest, we went fishing. There were no rods in the house, no tackle of any kind except an ancient sixpenny reel and a roach-line. We went out to buy tackle. For ten shillings we bought what were really two pieces of varnished wood, as rods ; we bought twopenny floats, twopenny lines, two-penny hooks, twopenny tins of shot. We dug worms, made paste, boiled handfuls of the ducks' wheat. The weather was magnificent, as it had been all summer, and as we went off to the lake, carrying baskets of lunch and tackle, I was reminded of those mornings a hundred years ago, described so beautifully by

Turgenev in "The Sportsman's Sketches," the hot, dewy mornings of Russian summers, when the grasses are golden with feathered seed, and the sky is clear with heat, and the distances, brown and white with corn, shimmer in the sun. That day, too, the corn was ripe and the ears shone like polished wood with the splendid sheen given only by weeks of sun and lost so quickly after rain. The orchards were purple-blue with plums, and by the waterside the loosestrife was glorious in sheaves of purple-red. The long, rainless summer had left the water of the lake low and clear, a golden colour, so that you could see everywhere on the bottom shoals of roach and perch marshalling and patrolling in the sun. By midday the heat was fierce and you were glad of the cool, sunless avenues under the alders, where the water was green and deep and unbroken except for the fall of a sun-turned leaf or the turn of a fish rising in the shadows. And as we sat down in the shade we were caught up by the deeply calming silence of trees and water, with its soothing-swooning effect, so that the sounds of the outside world, the sound of binders clacking in harvest fields, of gunfire on the sea-coast, of invisible planes and raid-sirens wailing continuously, seemed now like the sounds of an unreal world severed from the world of reality, the drowsy, silent world of the clouded August thorn.

I don't think I expected to catch many fish, but in two minutes the float was down. It was a perch, and after that there were roach. We fished all afternoon and about four lit a fire on the bank of the lake and had tea with the children, who had now arrived. The smell of tea and wood-smoke, the taste of butter warmed by sun, the voices of children, the flashing sun on the water, the poplars white-rippled by wind—they were parts of a free peace-time world, indestructible, very precious. But four o'clock was time, in these days, for the early evening raid to begin, and soon you could hear the high moan of invisible planes fighting somewhere at thirty thousand feet, and sometimes you would see them turn exactly as a fish turns and shows its silver flank in the sun. It was a new, fascinating element of fantasy in the world, and we stopped eating and drinking to look up. Eight in the morning, noon, four o'clock and perhaps six or seven in the evening were the programme times for battle, and it seems strange that even then we were growing so used to them day after day that soon we could turn away and fish again under the trees as if nothing had happened.

And under the trees I was making a proper fool of myself. Are you aware of what a fish-hook can do? It can get caught in trees, in grass-heads, in trouser-seats, in shirts and jackets; it can tangle with submerged wreckage, tree roots, old punts, lily roots, water-weeds; it can embed itself in the hair, the fingers, the ear-lobes, the back of the neck; it can take off hats and pull socks to pieces; it can get lost in the belly of a perch; it probably has an evil regard for beards and has probably pulled out innocent eyeballs; it has given rise to a painful expression of contempt— angling in all its branches—which is really the first lesson the despairing beginner learns, and which was the lesson I painfully learned on that August afternoon on a stream that, even for an expert, would require the most delicate casting and striking, as I have since discovered. Most of my fish that day were not only hooked but hanged. I hung them everywhere: round tree trunks, in high branches, round my legs and round my companion's neck. My method of striking was to give a rousing and gigantic pull, as if an anchor were being weighed, and hang the fish high in the nearest alder. Sometimes, since a path of only a yard wide separates the stream from the lake, I would strike and in a split second transfer the fish straight from one water into another. In spite of it all, I put five very fair fish in the bag and my brother-in-law a pair.

That hot August day something in me was touched which had lain dormant for thirty-five years.   I do not know how it is, but suddenly after half a lifetime you are impregnated with a new bacillus.   I dreamed of fish all that night, and in the morning I was digging worms before breakfast.   And later as we sat by the water a series of the most extraordinary incidents happened.   The morning was clear and beautiful, and out of the sun, under the trees, you could still feel the night coolness.   It was fresh and slightly stimulating, and beyond the shadows all the wet grasses were flashing in sun, rainbow-dropped.

In half an hour the battles began overhead.   We had not up to that moment caught a fish.   Normally we took little notice of battles in which there was no sound of machine-gun fire, and for a time we sat placidly fishing, listening to, but not troubling to watch, the planes zooming and whining somewhere far overhead in the hot morning sky.   Then machine-gun fire began very close, quite suddenly, and we ran out from under the shade of the trees in time to see a Messerschmidt falling rapidly by the woods.   We went back to the stream, and the rods were in the water : a pound roach on one hook and a pound perch on the other.   We baited up again, cast in, and waited.   Machine-gun fire broke suddenly over the woods again, coming nearer, and once more we left the rods and ran along the bank into open sunlight.   Soon there was a plane falling smokily in the sky, and soon we were back again by the water, where floats and rods were down and new roach and perch had hooked themselves.   This crazy business of falling planes and rising fish went on for almost an hour.   For centuries fish had been reputed lovers of silence and fishermen essential observers of silence, but now in this crazy and sinister battle there were fish which rose and fed to a new and appalling sound.

It was all part of the memorable hot beauty of that summer,

sharply impregnated by the prick of destruction : the clouded August thorn. It was a period of intense expectancy. The blue-white light of the searchlights swinging and climbing and crossing in the dark August night sky was sometimes so concentrated that the black woods and the empty cornlands were lit up as if by magnesium fire. As I stood watching their creeping triangular beams against the August stars I was reminded of the fireworks at the coronation of Edward VII when I was a little boy, when women carried frilled parasols and men wore boaters and white flannels with a stripe in them, when red, white and blue fairy-lights were hung in the limes and the chestnut-trees, and the bonfire of celebration cast upward a rosy-golden glow that has remained in my mind as the symbolic reflection of the easy prosperity of the age. It seemed to me that people grew a great deal more excited then than now. For now we stood out in the August darkness and watched the marshalling of the lights of battle in the sky with only a kind of stoical wonder. We were watching the lights of death, and as the crump of bombs and the stutter of the barrage began to the north-west we were listening to the sound of death. But we did not get excited. The nerves were like fiddle-strings which were being tightened a fraction more every day, just short of breaking-point, and on which the tune of conflict and destruction was being played a little more savagely every night.

I had never been a very patient person, but throughout these fantastic weeks of sky battles and night skies split by blue beams of searchlights I found myself cultivating patience by the simple process of dangling a worm in water and waiting for a small red float to disappear. For there is no doubt that fishing cultivates patience, rather in the same way as walking stimulates thought. Throughout the summer I had not worked much, though I was a normally industrious person. The war created nervous distrac-

tion, and the continued beauty of the summer weather and the
horror of war made a combination that stimulated cynicism. In
that sort of mood there could be, and was, no impulse towards
creation. But gradually fishing, and what has always been rather
pompously called communion with Nature, got back into my
veins the warm glow of confidence.

We had been warned by a friend of the dates on which an
invasion would be attempted. What he said was not gossip, but
rather more like the divulging of an Army secret. He was
quite right. On the specific date he came to spend a day with
us, and as we sat fishing that afternoon in the shade of a great
chestnut-tree, the water dead in the hot August air, the great
attack began. But before it began a curious thing happened.
In the hot silence there was suddenly a strange muffled sort of
report, like a toy gun going off in the reeds. It started us
very slightly, and then we smelled gas. It crept slowly across
the water, sinister as rotten eggs, and for a moment or two
we were really afraid. It was only when it dispersed that we
decided what it was: a coot's egg, addled by weeks of hot sun,
suddenly exploding.

But it was as if this rotten exploding egg were a signal.
Almost immediately afterwards, as we sat boiling the kettle over
a fire of dry wood, the planes began to come in from the coast.
Up to that day we had seen as many as eighty, a hundred, a
hundred and fifty planes flying over at one time. Now we saw
a phenomenon. It was like the inland migration of hundreds of
black and silver geese. They came in steadily and unceasingly,
not very high, the black geese the bombers, the silver the fighters.
The fighters made pretty circling movements of protection above
the bombers. They went forward relentlessly. The air was
heavy with moving thunder and the culminating earthquakes of
bombs dropped at a great distance. All that had happened before

that day now seemed by comparison very playful. The front line was being pushed forwards, and we at last were behind and not in front of it.

That afternoon many people were killed, many homes were wrecked for ever, and many nerves were broken. Yet when it had all passed and the migration of geese had returned and the sky was silent again, it was as difficult as ever to believe that a war had been in progress. The beauty of the clouded August thorn seemed quite untouched. Less than twelve months before, this same sunny, pastoral countryside had been filled with women and children coming down in hot trains from the East End. I had helped to meet them, driving a huge old Chrysler lent by a farmer, and now I remembered their one concern. All they wanted in those first days of war was not sanctuary but "How many shops you got in this village?"

"One."

"How many pubs?"

"One."

"Gor blimey!"

One shop, one pub, one great big hope! For them the countryside was from that moment damned. It did not matter that here they had the most beautiful country in the whole of Eastern England, that this land had been said by experts to be the richest in the world, that they were being housed and fed and protected in a world that was not only beautiful and safe, but in which hundreds of intelligent people found a way of life that approximated to their idea of a natural existence. Once the first reaction of fear had worn off, they began to drift back to the Mile End Road, until by the beginning of winter there were none of them left. And that afternoon of the inland migration of these hundreds of geese-like planes it was not so much of myself that I was thinking—for I went on fishing with stoical heartlessness—but of them. That afternoon they were losing their homes, their children and their lives.

Yet it was not possible to blame them for that return. They were going back, and wanted to go back, to what they felt was a natural life. They wanted shops, cinemas, pubs, buses, pavements to walk on. If they wanted the countryside, they wanted it with seats and shelters, in the form of a park. It was incredible to find that a huge section of our population were producing children who did not know how potatoes grew. The strange stories of evacuated children and their reaction to the countryside have become legends. Many, perhaps, were untrue; but many had a sad foundation in fact. War brought from the incredible districts of Eastern London a race of people whose way of living was a profound shock to the people of little provincial towns and of the country. These people recounted with horror stories of little boys who crept under the bed to sleep—"because our mum and dad always sleep on top"—of children who did not know the functions of plates and knives and forks, but ate with their hands.

Cobbett used to talk with great and bitter derision of the Wen, the impossible metropolis which, even in his day, seemed a false expression of existence. And as I travelled by train to London for the first time after that tragic Saturday and saw the mean and disgraceful homes along the railway tracks blasted to pieces or damaged beyond repair, I could not help feeling glad behind the bitterness. It was bitter to think of people, of tiny children, being killed; but there was a compensation in the fact that at least these same incredible slums were smashed and could never rise again. It was depressing to think of people living, loving and dying behind those damnably dirty walls; it was still more depressing to think that with proper education, proper direction, proper enlightenment, they, too, might have been safe among the chestnut

woods, the cherry orchards and the cornfields: the almost untouched world of mushrooms and meadow-sweet, of hops and
late honeysuckle, of Red Admirals and peacocks and tortoise-shells
and Painted Ladies on the purple flowers of buddleias, and of
kingfishers flashing among the nut-trees by the waterside—the
beautiful, imperishable world of the clouded August thorn.

VI

Strange Battlefields

I did not really begin to take great notice of the kingfishers until autumn. The calm, warm weather went on. Never oppressively hot, yet often cloudless day after day, it was the perfect summer. Apples grew scarlet on the trees of the Weald, and in September still there were trees heavy with black-purple plums. Melons ripened in the garden, and you gathered tomatoes once and sometimes twice every day. In the markets the finest plums were being sold for as little as eighteenpence for forty pounds. Single plants of petunia had reached four feet in diameter, and the willow-leaves were shrivelling yellow from the weeks of steady drought.

The kingfishers were part of this warm, lavish beauty. There is always something un-English about them. There is no other

English bird, not even the great spotted woodpecker, so brilliant: flashing blue enamel wings, under-breast of Indian copper. Even this tropical combination of colouring, if accompanied by desultory flight, might be merely charming. But the flight is fiery, direct, Spitfire-straight, so that this is really the fire-bird of England. Much of its beauty, too, comes from this same swift elusiveness: blue flash, thin cry, then nothing more to be seen or heard. The flight is so like blue fire, impossible to touch or capture, that it is rare to be able to watch a kingfisher. It is the split-second bird. You are caught unawares, and the eye records only the blue, swift spark of flight.

But that autumn and winter I discovered that it is possible to watch kingfishers. I discovered that they are creatures of fairly regular habit, with regular areas of patrol. So that whenever I had time to spare I would be by the lake, angling for a couple of hours for relaxation from work and raids, most generally in the afternoons. The most frequent visitors to the water during all that autumn and winter were coot, moor-hen, wild-duck, swans, herons, wrens and the kingfishers. All these, the swans and herons especially, were very irregular in habit. The swans would arrive and remain only for periods of a day or two, normally very dignified and aristocratic except on an amazing occasion I will describe later, and the herons were always shy and stand-offish, flapping heavily away at the most distant approach of strangers. It was the kingfishers that had, or seemed to have, such firmly fixed hours and habits. They could always be seen, and I do not think there was, that winter, more than one afternoon in ten when I did not see the blue flash of at least one patrolling bird. Moreover, they not only appeared at a regular time, but at a regular place at a regular time. I think they probably came most often straight downstream along the river, and most generally about three o'clock in the afternoon. They flew for two or three hundred yards downstream, turned across the lower lake, came back upstream, and then for some reason, halfway upstream, flashed away into the wood that comes down very thick to the edge of the water. This flight through the wood was a miracle. The wood is very thick low down, mostly of sturdy hazel and sweet-chestnut, so that a straight course through it looks impossible. Yet the course of the kingfisher never slackened in its pure flow of speed. It seemed to cut like blue light through the dark branches. Without effort it slid through and dissolved. The only evidence that it was still flying was the short, thin cry, not very beautiful but rather harsh and forlorn, repeated again and again, that in some way sharpened the silence of the dead winter afternoons by the still water.

And then time after time I would look up to see one of the kingfishers perched on the branches of a willow on an island in the lake. These branches, as winter went on, became more and more coloured until by February they were a varnished gold ; so that as it perched there the kingfisher had background and the blue of the wings was more than ever lit up. The hazels and the alders, too, began to break more and more warmly into colour until they were smothered with powdery gold and old tawny-purple gold. The alders hung in many places over the water, and at last on a day late in winter I looked up to see a kingfisher perched on an alder-branch close to my hand, breast turned towards me like a mirror of polished copper. I realized at that moment that the blue of a kingfisher is only half, perhaps less than half, of its beauty. For that upturned breast, in colour as shining as copper and as rich as an August tiger-lily, seemed to make ordinary even the magic fire-blue of the upper wings.

No change of weather, even hard frost, seemed to upset the kingfishers, and they remained a beautiful and regular part of the water-life throughout the winter. But it was in a period of hard frost that a very amazing thing happened to the swans. The lake had become the province that winter of two swans and four cygnets. The following spring the two swans reared a brood of eight cygnets, but during the winter the six birds were, for the most part, alone in the lake. One day I arrived to find the lake covered with a sheet of ice and peopled by six strange adult birds. Between these birds and the six resident birds there began that afternoon the most ferocious and comic ice-fight. It was like a battle of ice-planes. The two adult and four young swans were gathered at the lower end of the lake, moving on awkward and heavy feet across the new black ice. From the north came the invaders. They came down in a series of dive-bombing sweeps, necks outstretched, huge wings offensively magnificent. As they hit the ice they slid forward swiftly out of control, on their breasts, using their wings as brakes and their necks as spears of attack. They were relentless, returning again and again, slithering to attack on their breasts, beating their wings madly on the ice as they lost control. Now and then the resident birds, especially the young birds, were driven away, but whenever they came down to ice the strange swans attacked them again, giving them no rest. This attempt to drive them out and capture what had been their stronghold for many months went on all afternoon and had, in fact, been going on since early morning. There was something like comic ferocity about these huge white birds smashing down out of control on ice just strong enough to bear them. The noise of their immense wings beating the air and then beating the ice was a sound of quite considerable terror. The swift plane down was as rigidly controlled, as mechanically perfect, as the descent of a seaplane, and yet very much more beautiful. This battle for possession must have gone on until darkness, and I had no doubt it would be resumed in the morning. But in the morning a warm mist rose, and soon after daylight I heard above

64

The noise of their immense wings
beating the air and then beating the ice.

the mist the unmistakable sound of swan-flight going eastwards towards the coast, and when I went to the lake in the afternoon the two swans and four cygnets were in serene possession on the already iceless water, and the invaders had gone.

All this happened in winter, when the countryside is popularly dead and nothing ever happens. Several months earlier it had been necessary for me to leave the country and travel to London every day. All that time in the South the trains were very crowded, and soon, instead of being interested in birds and fish and falling planes, I became interested in people. It was good to make this change, to throw one sort of life into relief by living another, and then later come back to the old changing and yet quite changeless world of October leaves.

Already by that time the battalions of business men, travelling with the same cronies in the same compartments, regimentally pin-striped, hiding behind the barrage of "The Times," the roses of financial success in their buttonholes, had been much thinned out. In their place now were travelling the real battalions : tired soldiers going home on leave, tired soldiers coming back. The weather was very hot, and they carried loads of kit resembling those of porters on a tourist expedition, and I used to get into conversation by handing round the morning papers, which none of them ever seemed to buy. ("Nothing in 'em, anyway. All the same.") It was clear that most of them were in strange country. Far from home, they had no idea how long the journey would be, no idea of place-names, completely fogged as to how to get from Cannon Street to Paddington. One boy from Newcastle grew very excited on nearing London. Looking out of the window, he asked at every passing church, "Is that Big Ben?" and, when I told him no, I could see that for him it was a question of realizing a life's ambition. So, as we crossed the Thames, I pointed out St. Paul's instead, very impressive in the hot sunlight beyond the water. But he only shook his head, and I could see that it wasn't the same.

Soon I made a daily habit of it—getting into compartments crowded with soldiers, handing round the papers, getting them to talk about themselves, Dunkirk, the winter in France, giving what advice I could about crossing London. We were always crowded, always sitting on top of each other, always lively. Passing along the corridors, I would see officers, both men and women, sitting all alone in first-class state, bored, silent, out of touch. Sometimes there was a coincidence. Once I talked to a tough Regular Army sergeant who had served in India and China. I wanted very much to hear about that, but he talked as if it had been a trip to Brighton. Instead he talked about Bedford—there was a little village up there, Yelden, quite pretty, with a little thatch-roofed pub. He'd spent Sunday there. Very nice, but now he couldn't remember the name of the pub. Now, what was it? Damn it, what was it, now?

He couldn't remember, so I told him. "The Chequers," I said.

"Well, blimey," he said, "how'd you know?"

"My aunt kept it," I said, "for thirty years."

The making of friends had never been so easy. In the whole history of British railways there has never been, I should think, so much conversation and friendliness per mile as now. The air of silent refrigeration, the arid cross-examination of stares, the snoozing behind the fat peace-time blankets of newspapers—all that has gone. It has never been so easy to get all kinds of people to talk of themselves. I shall remember a long time the little Folkestone fruiterer—business gone to pot, three sons serving, all his army pension sunk, few prospects. His life should have been broken in half. Instead, never a word of complaint. And as if to show me what adversity really was, he told me reticently how, thanks to the last war, he had had thirty major operations on his stomach, and lifted his trousers' leg to show me a calf carved like a fantastic chair-leg by bullet-holes. In peace-time we should never have met. In an hour now he had opened his heart to me.

This sort of thing went on for a month. All the time the "blitzkrieg" was closing in on us. And yet all the time another curious thing was happening : evacuees from the coast were, in spite of everything, going back home. Two young women, the mother of one of them, and a frowsy brood of tiny children herded into the compartment on a suffocating afternoon. Dead tired from heat and travelling, they vowed and hoped, as long as they lived, never to go to Wales again. The babies grizzled and snuffled miserably, puffy-eyed, wet, hanging on laps like lumps of leaden dough. There was much threatening of bottom-smacking, alternate coddling, bottle-filling and despair ("If you don't be quiet that man'll come and git you"). The prettiness of one girl was still just visible, very dim, behind the dirty lines of poverty, weariness and a slight viciousness imposed by something at which I could only guess. "My God," she kept saying, "my God, my God," and I would have given my heart to know what lay behind it all.

Then changing circumstances turned me from the South. I began to travel North instead. The North of England begins, for me, on the platform of St. Pancras Station. A new life begins there : the Luton hat travellers with their samples, the downright level-headed boot-and-shoe men, the right-on-the-spot lads from Leicester eternally playing cards on outspread newspapers, the hurrying high-tea Yorkshiremen who demand "something more soobstantial" for tea. After years in the South it is impossible to mistake them.

Yet the very first afternoon I was, as they say in the Midlands, "sucked in." The man sitting opposite me looked like the pale, downtrodden city clerk who is a popular cliché in fiction. I had grown so used to interesting fellow-passengers that I was disappointed, and immediately read into the pallor, the neat dark suit and the air of weariness a life whose foundations were a desk, a semi-detached, a Morris-Ten, and a garden bounded by trelliswork. I was much mistaken.

In two minutes I was talking, not to a city clerk, but to a mining engineer home from the Gold Coast. The pallor had nothing to do with a city desk, but was the fruit of a climate whose humidity is too great to be measured, where nobody ever runs upstairs, where people conserve their strength by talking in whispers, and where all water is boiled. As the train went on I pumped hard. The working conditions, the natives, the social life, the colonial administration—I pumped out something about each of them. And lastly the gold itself. How was it worked, was there much of it, was it in danger of petering out? In answer he told me of mines in Ashanti that were too rich to be worked. "Daren't work 'em," he said. "We keep 'em under lock and key. Can't have too much gold in the world. Oh no, that wouldn't do."

Next day, in a world in which gold was kept under lock and key while homeless people starved and a nation struggled to find six million pounds a day for war, the train was crowded by people who literally no longer had a home. The tired young women with children I had seen going home to Dover were now repeated a hundred times. And not only young women, but old women, old men ("Look after him, porter; see that he gets out at Sheffield"), a boy with his rescued tabby-cat, whole families struggling as if on a bank holiday to get a seat on the overcrowded train. All needed sleep. There were more strange coincidences. I travelled twice with a man, the brother of a famous singer, before discovering his name was the same as my own. There was the country parson who, only the day before, I had found absorbed in the active restoration of his church, passionately reconstructing it with excellent taste, while in London the churches of centuries were being blasted to pieces. There were more cases of deceptive appearances—the little blonde office girl who had neither home, office, nor clothes, and on whom I almost took pity as destitute. She casually remarked as I left her that her fiancé was, or had been, a Dutch Cabinet Minister.

And finally there was the waiter in the restaurant car. I think of him as fighting for—indeed, risking his job for—democracy. The train, as always, was crowded; the tea, as always, bad, late and expensive. At one table a man was clearly not playing the game by trying to keep one seat for himself, one for his bag, and another for his overcoat. The waiter pointed out the injustice of this on a train where three hundred people were standing. The man made some objection in reply.

The waiter at once delivered a speech magnificent in its fire-eating anger. Didn't the gentleman know there was a war on? Didn't he know there were three hundred people standing on the train? Didn't he know how difficult travelling was? If he didn't, it was high time he did. Nor, said the waiter, need he think he could come on the train and throw his weight about. Times were difficult. People not only had not got seats, but many had not got homes. "And, finally," the waiter said, "not so much of your sauce, and not so much of your old-school-tie tactics. They'll get you nowhere here!"

Such a speech from waiter to customer struck us all completely dumb. It was the equivalent of a revolution, and was rightly regarded by all in the restaurant car as hot stuff. It was certainly something else that could never have happened in peace-time. In its way, dictated though it may have been by the weariness of the moment, it was a piece of high courage. In it spoke the souls of all waiters—and, I may say, a lot more of us besides.

As the daily exodus from London went on I found myself becoming interested in, sympathetic towards, attached to a great number of people. Death is a leveller; but death by bombing is, in more senses than one, the greatest leveller of all. It has smashed the silence of the English railway carriage.

By the time I got back permanently to the country the October leaves had fallen on the lake. On bright, calm days they lay in thousands on the darkening water, mostly yellow flotillas of poplar floating continuously down from great trees that themselves shook in the windless air with the sound of falling water, but on rainy days or after rain they seemed to swim or be driven away, and nothing remained to break the surface except the last of the olive-yellow lily-pads that in high summer had covered every inch of water like plates of emerald porcelain. The lilies had gone too, the yellow, small-headed kind that in bud are like swimming snakes, and the great reeds were going, woven by wind and frost into untidy basket islands under which coot and moor-hen skidded for cover at the sound of strangers.

All summer in this world of water-lilies the coot and moor-hen lived a bewildered life. There was no place where they could swim, and all day they could be seen walking daintily, heads slightly aside and slightly down, across the lily-hidden water, as bemused by the world of leaves as they had been in winter by the world of ice. In the clearer water they are more active. They dash madly up and down it, taking off and touching down like small, fussy, black seaplanes. Beside them the arrival of the wild-duck, at much higher speed, is almost majestic. They plane down, the necks of the drakes shining like royal green satin, with the air of squadrons coming in after long flights from home.

It was not until late summer that fishing was possible. The

71

water was so low and clear after drought that the fish could be seen in great dark shoals, sunning themselves, shy, impossible to catch. Only in the evenings, as the air cooled and the water darkened, and the surface was broken with the silver dances of the rising shoals, would you perhaps get a bite or two, a baby perch sucking at the worm, a roach no bigger than a sardine. All the time, on bright hot mornings especially, great pike would lie out in the middle of the lake in shoals of ten or even twenty, like black torpedoes, transfixed, never moving except in sudden, immense rises that rocked the water-surface with rings.

It is curious, but all the life on and about water seems to belong to water. Except for a solitary wren fidgeting delicately about the banks under the alder-trees, or a robin singing in the October afternoons across the water from the islands, all the bird-life is that of water-birds. Rooks never seem to come here, nor starlings; an occasional pigeon flaps across to the woods; even the sea-gulls belong to the ploughed land. But wild swans come back to nest in the piles of fawn-coloured reeds in the spring, and two great herons stalk the water-meadows every day, struggling ponderously upwards at the sound of voices. Snipe whirl away across the tussocks of brown-quilled sedge on the adjacent marshland, and a solitary kingfisher breaks with magic electric streaks the dark enclosures under the alders that span the narrowest water. But sometimes, and for long periods, there is no life and no sound at all. The water is slowly stilled after the last fish have broken it, the coot are silent, the leaves cease their shaking and falling in the dead October air. The crimson float comes to rest on water that seems to have on it a skin of oil.

On such still, clear days the colour is wonderful. From the south bank of the water poplar and alder and ash and horse-chestnut let fall high liquid curtains of lemon and bronze. Orchards of cherry and pear smoulder with drooping orange flames beyond the light wall of almost naked willows. The oaks are still green, but the beeches in the distances stand like red mountains. And on the lake itself unexpected colour springs up: an island of quince-trees, still green, but hung with many ripe lanterns of bright fruit that no one gathers.

On a Sunday morning, a little away from the lakeside, in the orchard, an old man with red cheeks and white hair fixes a ladder against a tree of pears. What year is it? It is not possible to tell. It is not possible to tell, that is, from the curtains of liquid colour that drip down into the lake, the glowing lemon quinces that are falling ungathered into the water, the orchard, the pear-tree, the old man testing with aged feet the set of the ladder, the sound of moving air stirring once again the slow detachments of bright yellow poplar leaves far up the water. It is quite impossible to tell. The beauty and atmosphere of water, the things that flourish on it and in it and about it, are quite timeless. So this might be 1840 or 1740; it might be a year when Gilbert White was recording the season at Selborne, when Kilvert was recording with naïve passion the young girls and the young springtimes of Victorian Clyo, when Walton, too, was holding a line in this autumn water and waiting for a touch. The silent lake, the turning leaves, the old man under the pear-tree, the float on the water, are words in a language all these men could understand.

There remain the things they could not have understood. Walton would have been puzzled by the behaviour of scores of fish which leapt high out of the lake after a tremendous and very close explosion on a still afternoon; Kilvert, used to hard Victorian winters, would have wondered about the stray snow-feathered circles and spirals and figures of eight drawn five miles up in the blue October sky, as if someone had been skating there; White would have been unable to identify the frequent flocks of high white birds, like celestial sea-gulls, or the twinkling metallic objects

73

that fly down into the water from nowhere, like a steel shower of dragon-flies.

None of them would have understood the thunder that shakes the earth on days when there obviously is no thunder, the moan and stutter of a sky that seems quite empty, or the object which suddenly flowers out of the sky like a giant convolvulus of pure white silk and floats down to rest somewhere on Kentish earth. None of them would have understood—and seeing the glowing quince-trees reflected in the calm, golden October lake among the dying lily-leaves you could excuse them for it—that this was a battlefield.

VII

The Great Snow

For the third year in succession winter fell on the same day. The long, wild, rainy autumn, the days of flying brown leaves herded by warm, wet sea-winds, broke at last on the Saturday before Christmas. The wind swung north, by afternoon it was very cold, by Sunday bitterly cold. By Monday the ponds were covered with ice that would bear, and by Tuesday there was snow. In 1939 it was snow such as no one had seen in England, so continuously at least and for so long, for fifty years and in many places for a hundred years.

That year there were many berries on the holly; in spring the trees everywhere had been covered by clusters of green-white, pink-touched blossom. There had been many berries, too, on the hawthorns, and there was a tree that stood claret-covered until the last week of December. The cold did not begin reluctantly, as it often does in England, but suddenly and bitterly and fiercely.

It bit down on the earth like teeth. It bit with a black and scarring effect, so that the earth seemed skinned raw by wind and frost and the trees were bared down to the black bone of the branches. Then it began to snow with that mournful, silent beauty, steadily and relentlessly, that only a great storm of snow can give. There are sometimes wild and brief snows which merely pepper the ploughed land into bars of whiteness and shadow. But this snow covered everything. It came down without a break for a whole day, then for another day, and then for still another. For seventy-two hours, day and night, it drove down on a bitter wind from a sky that seemed solid with dirty grey clouds as far as heaven itself. Almost always after great snow the sky clears. It becomes cloudless, more blue than summer, sun and snow dazzling as light from a flashed mirror. But now the sky showed no sign of clearing. The clouds remained thick and sombre, dirty as a vast sheepskin. For a day there was intense frost, then a thaw, then frost again, but the sky did not change. It remained always that sombre and dirty grey, as if it had in it a vast world of unfallen snow.

And everywhere the fallen snow was magnificent. Sometimes snow in England is a local story ; this snow was a national epic. It piled deep in the woods and lay like heavy froth on shrubs and trees. It filled to the brim the narrow roads that are carved in the steep sides of the downlands, so that they were still like rivers of snow running down the hill-sides long after the surrounding land was dark and unfrozen again and even touched with flowers. On the ridge below the downs it drove through the hedgerows as if through gauze, and piled up on the western and southern sides of them in vast elongated drifts that blocked lanes and roads like miniature ranges of snow alps. The shapes carved by wind driving falling snow, and then by wind driving in bitter misty blizzards the light powder-snow refined by frost, were of fantastic

76

splendour. They rolled away from the hedgerows like sea-waves of white marble. These waves were barbarously ridged, sharp-crusted, edges like knives. They were tipped with long and delicate curves which became overhanging eaves, making caves below. They were rippled like gigantic muscles of marble and into light branchings that were fringed like goose-feathers. They were as long and sharp as spears or as huge and deep and impassable as dunes of the purest snow-sand. Wherever there were turns of road in high places, a bank, a hedge, a fence on the corner of unsheltered land, these drifts were whipped by ground blizzards into barriers of fantastic and lovely marble.

At intervals it snowed again. The nights were bitter : thirty degrees, thirty-five degrees, almost up to forty. The lake, on which no one had skated for thirty years, was hard and solid as a billiard-table. For one-and-sixpence we bought two pairs of clumsy but excellent pre-Great War German skates for the two girls, then only seven and five, and in two days they were striking out. You could skate every day and all day, and you wondered what sort of skater you would make if winters like this were suddenly to come to England every year. You began to be proficient at back-skating, inside edges and outside edges. You began to try swallow glides and inside edges backwards. You began to be very proud. You rested on your skates and looked down into the thick, clear ice and saw the fish lying still under the ice, and you realized that for once you were freer in their own element than they were. Then you got a book on skating. It was Victorian and academic and classically high class. The skaters illustrated in the act of doing perfect inside edges looked like professors or country doctors or Dr. Grace laying down the law about the last ball of the over. You studied this book all evening and realized at the end of several hours that you could not skate at all. You never had been able to skate ; all you were doing was wrong. If any skater of ability at all were ever to see you skating, it was extremely likely he would die of apoplexy. You were simply a windmill. It would clearly be better if you were to forget all you ever thought you knew and begin all over again. So the next morning you took the book down to the ice. You put on your skates and consulted the book: page 47, Fig. 1, the forward inside edge. You carefully struck the correct attitude and prepared to proceed according to the highest Victorian standards in the art of figure-skating. You proceeded and promptly fell down and sprained your ankle.

That was the end of skating. The next day the snow came down fiercely and heavily again. Once more the blizzards drove through the hedges, piling up into the barbarous, beautiful drifts in the deep southern roads. And again, when the snow had fallen, the wind whipped it off the land in white salt-clouds that in turn piled into finer, sharper drifts. The sky still did not clear, but remained always the colour of a dirty sheepskin. It was now mid-January, and the holly-trees and hawthorns, scarlet and claret only a month before with a million berries, were now stripped black and naked. The birds were suffering greatly. Rooks herded together in oak-trees, holding funereal conferences on the strange state of emergency, sending out only an occasional solitary patrol to survey the land. Pigeons came down on the gardens, stripping every cabbage-stalk down to the level of the snow. It was hard to say what was happening to the smaller birds, but when spring came it was clear that thousands had died. There were fewer nests, and it was known that here and there whole species had been almost wiped out. But they were to suffer more than from frost and snow and ice-wind and blizzard. A phenomenon common enough on the American continent, but fairly rare in England—ice-rain—swept across the country, turning telegraph wires into cables of ice-rope, trees into skeletons of

In the country there was
also an effect of isolation.

glass.   It was at this time that birds were frozen to branches as they roosted or had their wings frozen to their bodies.

Between mid-January and the end of February there seemed to be scarcely a day when snow was not on the ground or falling or about to fall.   Winter in England is rarely continuous, but now it was continuous and deadly.   The English are bred to rapid climatic changes, and the snow, falling and lying for weeks on end, had a strange effect on character.   It made people at once raw, touchy and depressed.   Snow with sun, with the dazzling illumination that only sun and blue sky can give, is a bearable and beautiful thing, but now we had weeks of snow without sun, and the days had an imprisoning and unbearable effect.   In the country there was also an effect of isolation.   Buses ceased running, the arterial roads were beaten by traffic into corrugated switchbacks.   Snow-ploughs, horse-drawn or drawn, perhaps, by a slow orange tractor, drove passages along the secondary roads, and gangs of men cut gulleys where the snow-ploughs stopped. But no sooner were passages and gulleys cut than it snowed again, and finally, in the third-class roads and the lanes, the snow-ploughs ceased altogether.   Here the drifts remained piled above the hedges, high as the head of a man, untouched, in many cases, except by birds' feet or the three-pointed prints of rabbits.   Only the sun cleared them at last, many weeks later, and in the deep, sunless bends they remained unthawed until March.   Still later, on a warm, sunlit afternoon when the countryside was green again and the young winter-wheat was rising at last after weeks of snow, we drove towards the downs to look for primroses that bloom early there under the steep chalk banks in the shelter of giant beeches.   As I turned the car to take the deep, narrow road that runs up the hill-side, I stopped in amazement.   For there before me the drifts of snow, deep as the car-wheels, remained unmelted, shining like frosted glass in the sun.

VIII

A Summer Spring

That year it could almost be said that in England there was no spring. Winter lasted until March. Summer began on April the twenty-second.

On that day there came a sudden burst of warmth that opened all the creamy-green buds of the plum-trees to full flower. Primroses, already very late, now became huge, pink-stemmed. The oaks showed olive-brown. The effects of the winter began to be seen: in the leaves of the berryless hollies that were turned an artificial copper-grey, as if oxidized by frost, in the seared tobacco-brown cypresses everywhere, perhaps most of all in the thinned population of birds. Birds are small; they die insignificantly. For every one picked up frozen or starved to death a hundred, and probably more, die somewhere out of sight. That year, in our immediate locality, there certainly seemed fewer nests, yet it was impossible to say with accuracy how much the bird population had suffered. Certain species suffered more in one locality than another; there were large local decreases that could not hold good for the whole country. In a letter to me, R. M. Lockley even declared that he thought "the frost of early 1940 seems to have affected bird populations even less than the cold spells of 1917 and 1929." His reason for saying this was that, though birds do perish in great numbers in hard weather, the numbers are covered up in a short time, and that even starlings, which flock in great numbers to West Wales in hard weather, do not show any but an appreciable local diminution afterwards.

Yet, as Lockley said, the local suffering was sometimes severe, though it was often severe on the most unexpected species. You would expect it to be severe on such delicate creatures as buntings, woodlarks, skylarks, meadow pipits, wrens, robins and kingfishers, but hardly on such robust species as herons, wood-pigeons or plovers. Yet this, again, was quite reasonable when you remembered that, with every pond and lake and many rivers frozen, the food of herons would be almost unobtainable, that young corn, green vegetables and acorns, of which wood-pigeons are so fond in winter, would be deep under snow, and that marshland, pasture and ploughed land, so much foraged over by plovers, would be inaccessible for weeks on end. Small birds can live off the crumbs of doorsteps, but there is no similar sort of salvation for larger birds. Plovers, too, must have suffered, as they suffer even in normal winters, from the hostility of inland gulls, to whom life on ploughed land is softer, probably better fed and less harassed altogether than life on the coast. It is a common sight now to see gulls and plovers intermingled on ploughed land, so that occasionally, in certain angles of winter sunlight, it is hard to tell one from another, and it is also increasingly common to see gulls

With every pond and lake and many rivers frozen,
the food of herons would be almost unobtainable.

fiercely persecuting plovers, who apparently have no instinctive protection against a bird that has strayed out of or has enlarged its habitat. This fairly rapid and recent change in the distribution of gulls, which have tended to come farther and farther inland during this century, has been puzzling, and there is little doubt that plovers have suffered because of it.

According to Lockley, the species which suffered most severely during that amazing period when claws and tails were frozen to roosting-perches were long-tailed tits, gold-crests and Dartford warblers. He thought that probably the bearded tit had been almost exterminated. Yet still the cold had, apparently, not the severity of a period reputed by Gilbert White, who lived during several astonishing winters towards the end of the eighteenth century, and who recorded how "rooks, attempting to fly, fell from the trees with their wings frozen together."

And now, as spring advanced, birds began to suffer, if you could place any reliance on various reports, from something else. It was a common expression that spring, as the war began to intensify over Eastern France, and more still as it began to intensify over Eastern England, that "they don't like the raids at all." From the first I had the impression that this belief that birds were terrified, pained or in some other way upset by air raids was little more than an expression of the attitude that seeks to find for all animal activity a human standard of comparison. This is, of course, most noticeable and is carried to its extremest limits in the human attitude towards dogs, cats, canaries, parrots and other cage birds, which for their owners often replace human objects of affection once possessed but now lost, or never possessed and so continually desired. Petted animals often replace, in a good way or a bad way, children lost or never born. In the same way much of a desultory kind of interest in birds springs from the fact that in birds human behaviour can sometimes be seen in miniature, prettified. For many people a bird is not only small; it possesses a small mind through which small thoughts and desires, sometimes approximating closely to human thoughts and desires, seem to find expression. To such people it does not matter that though birds have " the hottest blood, the brightest colour and perhaps the strongest emotions of any group of animals," as James Fisher points out, " they are not very intelligent."

It was not surprising, therefore, to hear that " they don't like the raids at all," just as it was not surprising to hear that heavy gunfire caused heavy rain. Unfortunately for the last hypothesis, the heavy gunfire of spring, 1940, audible though it was all across Kent many hours a day for many days, coincided only with an unbroken spell of the most beautiful and rainless weather. It is obvious that birds are affected by heavy and unusual sounds. Storms and approaching storms have a disturbing effect on rooks and jackdaws. A gunshot, a blast from a quarry, will cause croaking alarm among pheasants, and an explosion of wings, like the delayed echo of an explosion, among a gathering of starlings at nightfall. Birds, like fish, are naturally ultra-sensitive to sound.

The question was whether birds were likely to be affected by the noise of aero engines and aerial gunfire reaching the earth from a height of twenty thousand or even thirty thousand feet. Lockley declared that birds get used to unusual sounds very quickly. Agitation among birds in springtime—as an expression of mating instinct alone, for example—is often considerable, and it began to seem very likely that persons watching the spring air raids noticed a coincident spring disturbance among mating birds and instantly connected one as the cause of the other. For me this idea was strengthened by the fact that though I am slightly more than normally observant and am especially sensitive to un-usually moving objects and sounds in the country, and though I was experiencing anything from one to ten air raids a day, I saw nothing that could be called raid reaction among birds. It was possible that examples of it were seen by other people, but it was also an interesting fact that persons who declared that " they don't like the raids" could never give the names of birds specifically or describe their reactions with accuracy.

It seems very unlikely, therefore, that birds were generally affected by raids, though they may have been affected on isolated occasions locally. They were certainly affected by bombs, which had on them much the same effect as the noise of quarry-blasts and sporting-guns ; and fish, as I have described, were also affected. The sight of many fish leaping out of the lake at the sound of a bomb is one which I shall not easily forget. But birds and raids formed, I think, an example of the attitude which seeks to humanize wild creatures. This attitude was bound to be identified with the feeling of concern or alarm or even distress at the thought that small birds might, like human beings, be suffering from the effect of sky-battles. There is some reason to believe that it might also have been a comforting thought.

So you got another example of how little a war, savagely though it was fought above the countryside, affected that country-side. The summer went on from that day in middle August as if the air-battles were not only clearing the sky of raiders, but clearing it also of cloud. But towards the end of the summer they began to do the opposite thing : they began to fill it with cloud. It was cloud such as had never been seen before. The white or blue-white vapour trails of plane-wings were a new phenomenon. They streamed in delicate smoke parallels from the wings of planes that were not visible, or they whitened sud-denly the fresh blue autumn surface of sky with soft splashes of milky curd. If there were many planes and the sky was blue and clear enough, it would be as if the sky were ice and the planes were skaters marking on the virgin surface all the rings and spirals and figures-of-eight and fancy cuttings that skates make on a frozen pond. These patterns, sharp, frost-white, so fine and fancy when first made, added something to the history of clouds. Sometimes you never saw the planes except for a split second as they turned in the sun; all you saw were the parallel streams of snow pouring backward from a moving point. Sometimes a squadron would turn in the sky, and then the snow-trails would turn too, suddenly merged together or split apart, but always, as they hung far behind, enlarging and softening and sometimes even assuming the shape of natural cloud, remaining visible for a long time.

That autumn, when the weather broke, there was still another phenomenon in the sky. I am not quite sure now when the summer broke, but November was smashed by gales and drenched by days of heavy rain. Cloud was no longer the creation of plane-wings. Clouds themselves were now squadrons driving inland from the sea on high, squally south-west winds that disturbed in the brown, sapless leaves the echo of sea-sounds. Sometimes it would rain all night and then all morning, and then the sky would clear in the afternoon. It was about then, in the late afternoon or very early evening, that the sun-dogs appeared.

A sun-dog is a kind of rainbow ball, soft, cloudily iridescent, that invariably seems to appear a little to the right of the sun. Its appearance is said to be a forecast of rain within three days, and certainly that autumn it was never wrong. It appeared almost every day, like a fragment of floating rainbow, remaining visible for several minutes or for as long as half an hour. This was remarkable enough, since I could recall having seen it only once before. But now quite frequently there was an imitation phenomenon: the sun-dog of the dog-fight. Now and then it seemed that a burst of petrol vapour or perhaps oil was caught and held at the edge of a cloud or was large enough to form a separate cloud itself. This rainbow vaporization produced exactly the effect of the sun-dog, so that often it was not possible to tell one from the other. Only the plane vapour seemed slightly brighter, faintly unreal and rather ominous. The sun-dog foretold rain; it always seemed as if the sun-dog of the dog-fight might foretell or even record disaster. It was a new kind of sky-omen, still another freak of sky-beauty which no age but our own had ever seen. And it was strange that after the rainy weather ceased we never saw either the old or the new sun-dog again.

IX

"... *Bring forth May Flowers*"

Again, for the second year in succession, winter began on the same day. This year there were no holly-berries, but soon, by New Year's Day, the cold was intense and the blizzards had begun again. It was as if time had gone back and this were the old bitter record winter repeated. Once again the drifts were thrown fantastically, serene and smooth as marble, across the deep roads of the South, and once more they were fringed and hollowed and razor-edge as they piled up on unsheltered corners and through wire fences. Once more there was skating and ice-rain, and once more birds were frozen to branches. There were again sunsets of appalling splendour in which the sun went down like a lump of red-hot iron just cooling and falling towards an horizon of leaden bitterness. There was a day when the snow turned yellow, the creamy-yellow of beef-fat, and another when a blizzard of light earth blown off the ploughed lands turned it a light coffee-brown.

All of us were in despair at the prospect of a new hard winter. I noticed especially one interesting thing. Most of my life I had been listening to older people talking reminiscently and rather fondly, I thought, of severe Victorian winters. From these people you got the impression that winter descended on the countryside year after year with splendid severity. Drifts of snow were piled over the hedge-tops, rivers were frozen solid, men skated for eighty miles without a break. Moreover, you got the impression that a very good time was had by all ; all was jolly and hearty. There were fires on the ice and rum-punch in the parlour. There were hot chestnuts in every street and steaming sirloins on every table. Those winters produced a very hardy race of folk who now, in later middle age, slapped their chests and did not conceal a mild contempt for later generations who had not the slightest notion of what winter really was.

Now at last we knew what winter was. We were presented, first, with the coldest winter for a hundred years, and then, twelve months later, with a repetition so exact, during the period it lasted, that it was uncanny. Now, it seemed, the late Victorians had what they wanted. Unfortunately, it seemed that it was not quite the same sort of cold they had in the nineties. It was then a drier cold ; or it was a sunnier cold. There was better skating ; you could keep warmer. It was not this wet, hateful, biting cold ; it was not this stabbing raw cold that got into the bones. In fact, they were all very miserable. They did not now slap their chests or talk of softer generations. Instead, I noticed that they did not take off their slippers for days, and that the only sign of that robust energy which had once taken them whizzing over miles of frozen rivers was seen in a rather fretful stoking of the radiators.

For myself I was between two affections. Either I wanted it to freeze more so that I could skate, or I wanted it to freeze less so that I could fish. For fishing, which I had hitherto regarded as an entirely summer pursuit followed mostly on hot days in the shade of willow-trees, had continued to keep me sane and hardy throughout the winter. As the days grew colder I began to fish for pike. I had not the slightest notion, at first, how this was done, and I read up the whole subject in a Victorian manual in which there was a painfully personal illustration called " Angling in All its Branches." I decided to fish with live-bait and then with a spinner. After buying a very handsome scarlet and silver spinner, I took up the position recommended in the manual. From this position I proposed to make a cast across the lake, and it seemed very easy. I swung the line several times backwards and forwards and then let go. Very much to my astonishment, I almost hanged myself in the nearest tree.

Perseverance and patience are virtues I have never pretended to have, and which no one who knows me would believe are even potential qualities. Now they were revealed as the basis of my whole character. I persevered in the face of the most difficult complications. The hooks got into my clothes, my hands and my boots. The line tangled itself in trees and in the frost-browned stems of chicory that had once been beautifully blue on the lake-edge. The spinner would not spin. Though I perse-vered and was patient, I had no one to tell me what to do. But, as in most things, one becomes proficient through an oppressive series of mistakes, and at last I taught myself how to make a cast of thirty or forty yards with fair artistry and ease. This meant that I could spin across two-thirds of the lake. It was only then that I discovered that the lake was too weedy for good spinning and that the pike, too well fed, would hardly look at a spinner at all.

There is something terrifying and relentless about a pike. I do not know if the word " cruelty " can be applied, in its human sense, to birds or animals. It is common to suppose that stoats and weasels are cruel, and that even spiders are cruel, whereas these creatures are simply obeying a natural law governing survival. But R. G. Walmsley has described in " Winged Company " how he watched a great black-headed gull " very slowly doing to death a young shag or cormorant by gently and intermittently crushing

its neck within the vice of its great yellow beak.'' A pike sometimes reveals some of the qualities of that gull. It possesses
natural power which enables it, when it chooses, to impose on
weaker creatures a process of what seems to be purposely prolonged
pain. Whether this can be called cruelty is doubtful, but I have
seen a pike worrying a fish very much as a dog worries a bone,
and the number of roach which show signs of having been ripped
or scaled by pike is very great. It is not only because of his size
that a pike looks a forbidding and demoniac creature. The mouth
is enormous—I suppose a six-pound pike could get into its mouth
the larger part of an average adult hand—and, like the shark's, is
low in the underside of the head. The impression of stream-
lining, power and demoniac relentlessness given by this mouth,
whether closed or open, is immense. A pike, indeed, arouses
curious feelings of enmity for which I personally know of no
parallel among English wild creatures.

When a pike rises out of the water, as they used to rise very
frequently on those trying afternoons when I was learning to spin,
the impression of power—more, perhaps, of surplus power—is
again great. Later I learned to drop in a line quickly at places
where a rise had taken place, and very often I hooked a fish. But
at first it was hard to get bait, and it was not until I baited with a
goldfish one winter afternoon that I had my first real run across
the lake, and then was not sure what to do with it. I struck hard
and excitedly and, as it happened, at the correct moment, and I
felt the fish play on the end of the line like a moving house. I
saw him turn in the water like a steel band whipped to an arc and
then dive straight again. At that moment the twenty-pound-
strain line snapped like sewing cotton above the float, which
bobbed to the surface and became still. I wound in the line and
was then astonished to see the float moving with gathering speed
across the lake. It suddenly dived and came up again and then

*It is not only because of his size that a
pike looks a forbidding and demoniac creature.*

shot off again like a scarlet bullet. It went on diving and re-appearing and shooting off like this all afternoon until at last it became motionless in a patch of water-weed.

I think this fish will always be for me the biggest in the world. Later I landed other pike, as many as seven in an afternoon, but I shall always see that pike turning like a steel arch, whipped by fury, and breaking my strongest line like cotton. Later there was another pike which frightened me. Though he weighed only five pounds, a weight at which many anglers reject a fish, he ran furiously. It was warm weather and it was as if the heat had sent him slightly crazy. At the very last moment he rose clear out of the water, bent like a steel spring, furious. I landed him with some difficulty, and then, as the gentleman is reputed to have said in an old fishing story, he ran at me. I thought for a moment he would bite my legs. He rose up in the air in a series of attacking leaps, very strong and vicious, until suddenly I felt that it was he and not I who was master by force. I suddenly realized I had no natural defence against this creature, even out of its element. It was an extraordinary thing that I could not kill it except by an acquired weapon. I could not bite it with my teeth or strangle it with my hands or crush it with my foot. I was nearly thirty times as heavy, but I had relatively less power, and I could not use it. All I could do was to strike it hard on the head with the handiest stick, and when I had done so I felt tired with the shock of relief. The spectacle and impression of natural power in that savage fish was more forbidding than the behaviour of any other creature I had ever seen, and as soon as I had caught it I packed up my things and went home. For almost the first time after catching a fish I did not want to go on fishing.

There are stories of pike attacking men, and the fish, especially in Ireland, is altogether a legendary creature. It is quite natural, of course, that all lost fish should look larger than those which are landed, for water has a certain power of magnifying, and a fish turning in the water often looks double its size. A perch has some of the lusty greed of a pike on a smaller scale, and you will find anglers that will not pick up a perch. They hate the steely comb of the back-fin that rises with porcupine fierceness at danger. But the perch is really pretty : bright olive skin, darker stripes, scarlet fins, blue lip, and the spawning habit is attractive. You will find perch-spawn woven like scarves of creamy transparent silk among the spring reeds, and, if the water is warm and the spawn has been fertilized by the male milt, you may see the minute double-dotted eyefish just hatching out in the jelly and giving a birth-dance, flipping their minute bodies free of jelly and then rising to the water surface, more minute and more transparent than tadpoles, incessantly wriggling up and down when they are finally free. Later these minute fish sometimes blacken the summer water in thousands, so that the under-surface suddenly will seem to shudder with a moving shoal of tiny fins.

By the time the perch are spawning, the bluebells are in flower in the long wood that comes down to the edge of the water. In 1940 there was only a brief spring : almost, as I have said, no spring at all. In 1941 there was also no spring ; the period from March to early June was reputed to be the coldest for a hundred years. It has been said that periods of war are accompanied by exceptional periods of weather. Exactly how one of these mani- festations accounts for the other I don't know ; nor, I should say, does anyone else. But it is true to say that almost all the weather of 1940 and 1941 has been phenomenal : the two terrible winters, the miraculous long, temperate summer of 1940, the bitter spring of 1941, and now, as I write, the great heat-wave of 1941. By the end of the first week in June the days of summery spring could be counted on the fingers of one hand. By the end of the first week in July a month of great heat was unbroken. The hay, enriched by earlier rain, now ripened too fast for the mowers. It seeded and turned dry and blonde under a sun that began to colour the oats with a touch of fawn-silver early in July. There was a day when the heat haze was like coppery smoke on the horizon and when the heat struck down, as it rarely does in England, like the hot, flat blade of a knife.

Even by the waterside now it was hot, and the water itself had a thick odour very like that of seaweed drying in the sun; but it was like moving into cool water to walk out of the sun into the woodland, where the bracken was high as a man under the birch-trees, and strawberry-fragrant in the shade. It was so hot that even the snakes were swimming in the river running on the cool side of the wood; the sweet-chestnuts were in full blossom, with long spires of olive-green flower, oversweet and heavy in the windless air; there was hardly a bird voice or an animal moving, except the swimming snakes and a pretty dark vole foraging like a miniature beaver along the river-bank, and now and then diving out of sight; there were big silver-washed fritillary butterflies on the oak-leaves, and there were dewberries in flower under the floating cream trails of honeysuckle, but the red campions were dried in the heat, and the bluebells were only stalks now of parched and naked seed.

Whatever the spring, the bluebells are always magnificent. Nothing can stop them. They begin to spear up as early as February, sharp leaf-points pricking clean through the flat fawn skeletons of dead sweet-chestnut leaves, sometimes uplifting them completely, making miniature awnings under whose shadow still other leaves pale and sicken to the colour of straw. The strength of this upward movement of countless spearing leaves is immense; the whole floor of the wood rises, moved as by no other flower throughout the year.

Primroses, by their flatness, seem to make the earth itself

flatter ; they give the impression of having been scattered casually down. The bluebells are a force, rising in mass obedience to the magnetism of early summer light.

For the English there is only one bluebell, officially known, for some reason, as *Scilla nonscripta*, though we possess another, rarer and smaller, *Scilla verna*, the spring squill, found sometimes in coastal pastures. The bluebells of Scotland are something quite different : the little summer harebells of the moors. The name for both is wrong, since there is no pure blue in either, and in harebells nothing to do with hares. Bluebell is the homely word ; but wild hyacinth gives an impression of slenderness and delicacy, with a touch of Grecian warmth that seems to fit more perfectly the commonest aristocrat of all English flowers.

There are more than 2,000 species of English native plants, but few of them startle the landscape with their profusion. Daisies and cowslips in April, buttercups in May, moon-daisies in June, poppies in July, willow-herb in August—there are few others. We have no September meadows of crocus; no spring fields of grape hyacinth and narcissi, and these few mass flowers of ours, with the exception of cowslips, lack a touch of aristocracy. Daisies and buttercups and willow-herb are scentless, moon-daisies and poppies harshly odoured. Only cowslips have the charm of a scent so sweet that it can be tasted, so that a real cowslip-field such as you see often in the flat lands of Huntingdonshire, deep and thick with heavy flowers of almost orange-gold, is still by far the sweetest of English fields, a joyful and glorious thing, part of the sun.

But bluebells are not of the sun. Cowslips are bland and friendly and sweet, open-hearted, whereas there is something about bluebells, growing away from the sun, under rapidly thickening trees, their colour so intermediate and delicate that it seems sometimes to be part of sky and space, that is eternally elusive.

97

IN THE HEART OF THE COUNTRY

In February and March they lift the floor of the wood with thousands of glassy bright sharp leaves, but by late April or early May, when they are coming into their full glory of flower, they seem no longer to belong to earth. The earth now has lifted them, so that they are massed in misty suspense above it, like stretches of low mauve cloud, almost like mauve smoke, thinning and thickening about the feet of the trees.

By early May the English wood is at its best. Wild cherries are white above the yellow masses of leafing oaks; the new leaves of beech and sweet-chestnut have an almost transparent delicacy; the shadows are being stitched together, but the light still falls through the trees like golden lace. In marshy places the kingcups are almost over, but the grey, smooth spears of the wild yellow irises are rising above the fallen flowers. The wild anemones have almost gone, and the last of the primroses, but the pink and purple fingers of the first wild orchis are rising everywhere from among chocolate-spotted leaves; and now, everywhere, all through the wood, through and beyond the edge of unfurling bracken, into fields and under hedges and beyond ditches and so to the roadside, the bluebells have spread their flowers like ears of drooping purple corn.

And it is difficult now—in fact, impossible—to believe that they are dying out. They seem as indomitable as grass. Walking among them seems as wrong as treading through a field of corn. In a foot of earth there are hundreds of bulbs, white, from the size of peas to the size of a decent pippin. And sometimes, perhaps under a sheltered arch of dead bracken plaited by wind, the seeds of last year's flowers are sprouting as they fell, thick as grass, as one sees split corn sprouting sometimes in a farm-yard.

Soil seems to make no difference to this prodigious seeding and flowering. On the bare, hungry chalk of the hill-side woods the bluebells seem thicker, and even slightly earlier, than those in the dark, rich soil of the valley below.

And now, for two or three weeks, they outshine and outscent any other flower. On warm afternoons that heavy but still in some way elusive hyacinth fragrance will be driven out of the woods on a south wind, drowsily intoxicating, thickening and evaporating exactly as the colour of the flowers pales and darkens, in waves, under the sun-broken trees.

It is a glory that I only once saw challenged by another flower. That year the young chestnuts of a wood had been cut down, leaving the bluebells to flower in wide lakes among standing oak and birch. The sudden letting in of light disturbed a million dormant seeds of pink campion. They sprang up everywhere among the bluebells, making a thick blending of pink and mauve, broken only by rarer candle-bells of the pure white hyacinths. For a time it seemed as if the bluebells must be out-seeded and out-flowered. But the next year, for some reason, every campion had gone.

X

Victorian Garden

Looking back into childhood, I remember August gardens with affection. There used to be a garden enclosed by stone walls above the white cliffs of a stone-pit, which had been planted with fruit trees and was sheltered on the far side with pines. The house was kept by an old lady with a thousand-and-one dogs, and we went there in August at fruit-time. Whenever I read the country stories of Turgenev, with their settings of country houses, dogs, sleepy orchards and the dew of summer on the grass, I think of this house. It comes back to me as a period piece of the year 1840, or perhaps 1850, or 1870; it hardly matters. You have seen it as the setting for "The Cherry Orchard"; you have come across it, perhaps, in Trollope; you have seen its counterpart in the films of the American Civil War. It was square, stone, flat, unpretentious. There was a verandah, on which the thousand-and-one dogs and the few tortoise-shell cats went to sleep. Venetian blinds of pale coffee colour were lowered on hot August afternoons; a cream and crimson sun-curtain hung at the front door, flapping above red pots of blue agapanthus flowers on the porch. Round the garden there was a high stone wall, and round the walls were fields of corn; but within the wall, and perhaps even more within the walls of the house, there was an atmosphere which went back beyond the American Civil War, the Crimea, the accession of Queen Victoria, and even perhaps beyond the beginning of the nineteenth century. It was atmosphere that was not merely a compound of associations; it was an atmosphere in reality, an air, a definite but indefinable odour. It had something to do with mahogany furniture, with the moulded white cornices of drawing-rooms, with silver-watered wallpaper, with curtains of heavy strawberry rep at the windows; it had much to do with the odour of heavy carpets, of paraffin lamps, the smell of linen, the queer but pleasant smell of sun-warmed dust and sun-warmed air of closed rooms; it had something to do with comfort and a modest prosperity; and in August it had, above all, something to do with the fragrance of fruit and flowers that poured into the shadowy rooms from the garden outside. It seemed like an atmosphere which had been constant, perhaps unchanged for fifty or a hundred years; you could not tell; it had, perhaps, not changed since Gilbert White pottered round those prolific August cucumber frames at Selborne.

This garden was much less remarkable for flowers than fruit. Yet its flowers stand out in memory. I see large red satin hollyhocks by the wall, cream roses—perhaps Gloire de Dijon and William Allen Richardson—on the house. There is a greenhouse: a scarlet flash of amaryllis through the glass. There is a green rose on the lawn. And through the trees in August the glorious orange trumpets of vegetable marrows glow underneath the silvery branches of honesty that are hung with papery seeds. The larkspurs are bright blue against the scarlet arches of runner beans; the gaillardias are as if cut out of scarlet and orange Indian blankets. Old phloxes, small-flowered, mauvy-pink, dead white, are scattered among blue cornflowers. The colours everywhere are wrong according to correct standards, and yet somehow right. Orange and lemon and tangerine and occasional cream nasturtiums cover the ground under the old Victoria plum-trees; the African marigolds are like orange sponges, strong and almost harsh in the sun; the scarlet geraniums are spilt like blood on the distances. But above everything stand the dahlias: pot-hatted, huge, commanding. In some quarters they are despised. From this garden I recall a great lemon cactus like a giant yellow sea-anemone that had something Chinese about it; I see the stiff Victorian little pompons, like mauve and crimson and speckled honeycomb; the fat, flamboyant doubles like scarlet suns. The whole garden is a jumble, ill-planned; trees and flowers grow together; the yellow August plums, carved down to the stone by wasps, fall among the pinks, the catmint, the flowerless arabis; sunflowers rise far above the apricots on the high south wall.

Over everything there is a smell of ripened corn and fruit and dead-ripe grass, all the warm juiciness of late summer. In the hollow of the stone-pit, where the trees have struggled up to a great height, there is a smell of pines on heavy days; the pears are columns of gold. There is a small, pure yellow plum, rather square, turning when fully ripe to the reddish-gold shade of an apricot, that comes in with harvest. You split it open with your fingers, and it falls in half as if cut by a knife—clean, running with golden juice, aromatic and sweet like thin honey. Siberian crabs are filling out to the size of cherries, and will later turn even

he scarlet geraniums are spilt like blood on the
stances. But above everything stand the dahlias.

more scarlet; the Bramleys and the Blenheims strain down heavily against the props under their branches. Everywhere there are fallen plums in the grass, the savage hum of wasps, big peacock butterflies, drowsy on leaves and flowers. There are still a few golden gooseberries that you can crush on your palate like grapes, feeling the spurt of half-sweet seeds on your tongue. There are still a few raspberries, but mostly the birds have torn away the pink flesh, leaving only bare white nipples among the leaves. There are still a few red currants and a few white, perhaps, under the creamy ragged bird-scares that look as if they had been cut out of the old lady's chemise. The asparagus has a touch of gold; the cucumbers curve like green bananas. If there has been a wind in the night, you crush fallen fruit wherever you walk, and the old lady walks with you, quaking and whittling and muttering what a shame it is, what a shame, and the thousand-and-one dogs walk with the old lady, sniffing in the golden grass among the fallen fruit for the smell of a rabbit. Everything, from the fattest Bramley on the highest bough down to the rottenest honey-combed pear in the grass, is sacred. Everything is precious; everything is wrong. The fruit is glorious, but the wind blows it down. The fruit hangs on, but is eaten by wasps and birds. The weather is dull and the wasps are scarce; you hire a man to shoot the birds; but somehow the boys have been over the wall again, and—oh, dear! oh, dear! what are we going to do?

The old lady is deaf and talks in a whisper. She quakes so much you think her hands will drop off. There is a bit of a moustache on her lip, and she wears a pocket on a black silk cord. It is the time of the last war: no air-battles, no parachutes, no sky-battles, not even the sound of guns. It is 1915 or 1815 or perhaps even 1715; in that sun-soaked garden in mid-August you could never tell. There is trouble in the world, but it means nothing. All the trouble in the world will not equal the trouble of gathering the fruit, combating the wasps, thwarting the scrumping boys. The old lady quivers and quakes throughout the long tour of fruit-scattered grass, hand to ear, striking sometimes at the dogs with the cord of her purse, shaking her head, bowed down by trouble. Beyond the wall the corn has been cut, and now the rooks are on the corn. No business of hers, of course, but—oh, dear! oh, dear! more trouble. From time to time it is necessary for the old lady to be bellowed at, and this sound hits the air like the echo of a gunshot, startling a flock of starlings from the farthest tree of pears. More trouble! The Lord giveth, but the Lord taketh away.

The old lady and the dogs dissolve at last into the mellow distances. The deep August silence, amplified by the sound of wasps that seem to be burning their way everywhere into fallen and unfallen fruit, comes down again, heavy and drugging. It is hot in the hollow against the limestone. On the stony ledges, which suit the fruit-trees so well, there are dwarf thistles, mauve scabious, many butterflies. I do not seem to recall a buddleia in the garden, but, if it was there, it, too, would be covered in August with Tortoise-shells, Painted Ladies, Red Admirals, Peacocks. Moths would charge softly through the August dusk as we gave up at last the gathering of fruit and went back to the house, to pick up again that atmosphere of dust warmed by sun throughout the hot day, the smell of dogs, of paraffin and candles; the air of linen and mahogany; the air of comfort that should be trivial but is for some reason persistent and perhaps imperishable. The moths fly into the house, towards the lamp, from the silent garden; they are heavy, fur-brown, dusted; or they are cream, pure milk-white, delicate, like thistledown. The scent of tobacco-flowers is strong on the evening air; the leaves of the house geraniums are strong-odoured. The dogs lie under the tables, quiet after the day, and the white horse that is waiting for us outside, tethered to the verandah-post, begins to look vague, like cotton, as I look out of the window into the falling darkness. There seem to be many clocks in the house, and they strike ten one after another. There is a dark plum cake on the plush tablecloth under the ornate brass lamp, and a glass of rose-coloured rhubarb wine.

This old, dark house, with the coffee-coloured Venetian blinds and the garden rich with fruit and untidy with flowers, probably accounts for my affection for August gardens; and because we never went there except when the weather was fine or was going to be fine there remains a constant happy impression of heat and sunlight. It was a large, beautiful, half-wild paradise. Yet it lacked some of the things which should be part of all August gardens. I try to recall tiger-lilies, but without success; there are no zinnias, which were not much in fashion then; no petunias, as there ought to have been; no ten-week stocks; no ostrich asters. Most of all, perhaps, there should be asters. They belong to the Edwardian period, and express it, as perhaps no other flower does. They are blowsy, feathery, curly mopped; the deep purples, the silky pinks, the lacy mauves, the bosomy whites, recall quite vividly the ladies of a period when long white gloves covered their arms and high-neck frills were fashionable, and when boas and ostrich feathers were, as they used to say then, all the go. Taste in clothes and flowers is more stream-lined now. Ostrich feathers have gone, and with them, almost, ostrich asters. Summer being a kind of lottery in England, it was never certain how soon the ostrich feather would cease looking like a meringue and begin looking like a helping of cold bread sauce. So with the asters. They were like feathers in the sun, foamy and delicate; rain turned them to saddened puddings nutmegged with earth. There is a variety now called peony-flowered, finer, more delicate, incurved. The ostrich flower was fluttery, feminine, collapsible. The peony flower is self-supporting. In the two flowers you can see two types of womanhood separated by forty years of time, and the change in a dozen aspects of taste reflected in them.

It is interesting how the taste and fashions of a period get reflected in flowers, and when I was a boy August gardens were more flamboyant and high-coloured, I think, than they are today. The prevailing mode, as with ladies, was a bosom effect. To this both asters and dahlias, and later chrysanthemums, were admirably suited. Clouds of gypsophila broke up with almost transparent delicacy the stagy backgrounds of plush-crimson and magenta and soldier-scarlet, the shop-window foregrounds of boa vermilions and mauves. The age was competitive. Every gardener kept a secret store of vintage liquid manure in a sunken barrel behind the greenhouse, and from it drew reverent supplies that fattened the dahlias like prize hogs. Rulers came into play in August in order to measure the vast flowery diameters. The hats of the period and the flowers of the summer were remarkably alike, just as the Canterbury bells showed a remarkable similarity to the famous frilled bloomers of the time.

In August there were also carnations. They had the elegancy of the period: sophisticated, fragrant, well mannered, the emblems of aristocracy. It is interesting to see how a flower, beginning as nothing but part of a system for the reproduction of its species, can gradually come to stand for the expression of a particular human characteristic: arum lilies for death, carnations for pleasure and aristocracy and festivity, camellias for passion, orchids for affluence. A pineapple is a splendid fruit—exotic, decorative, a piece of fruit sculpture—yet it does not mean anything. Giving it to a lady, you could explain with enthusiasm its high vitamin content, its peculiar beauty, the romance of its passage from Hawaii. You could indicate that you wished to imply that the seductive sweetness of it had a counterpart only in the sweet seduction of the lady. You might just as well give her a brick and draw the analogy that your character, your bank balance and your goodness of heart were just as sound and solid. But, giving a carnation, you need say nothing. The flower implies all the things that need be said, that have been left unsaid, that cannot be said.

Forty years ago they were undoubtedly rather more generous, more gallant and less self-conscious about flowers. It was not regarded as vulgar to grow dahlias as large as hats, sunflowers like vast cheese-cakes, asters like feather ruffles, any more than it was regarded as "pansy" for a man to wear a buttonhole. The standard of buttonholes was then very high, especially Sunday buttonholes. It has been explained by psychologists that the city man who wears a rose in his lapel every morning as he goes to town does so not because he is fond of roses, but because he is subconsciously aware of being, as a character, below a certain standard of strength or achievement. The rose, because it will attract attention, because it seems to indicate elegance and affluence, will raise him up, in his own estimation and, he hopes, in the estimation of others, to that level and perhaps above it.

How it is possible to apply this to the buttonholes of forty years ago I do not know. They seem to have reached their most prolific development in August, when sweet-peas, carnations, asters, gypsophila and pompon dahlias were in bloom. All these, garnished with maidenhair, were great favourites. The word for the effect they made, perhaps, is "luscious." They were expansive. They transformed a man from a man into—here, perhaps is the better word, after all—a toff. In that sense, perhaps, the reasoning of the psychologists is quite applicable. For one day a week, on Sunday, for a few hours a man was lifted up from the plain weekday levels to the high levels of aristocracy by the simple process of wearing a bunch of flowers. How pleasant and charming that simple psychological remedy was!

Whenever I see August gardens now I think of these button-holes. I fancy the gardens of today are more orderly, more subdued, less restricted in pattern and variety. Stocks and asters were once as holy as the Apostles' Creed. Now as I look across my own August garden, where an almost white-breasted thrush is dividing its time between the plum-blue berries of the berberis and listening with side-cocked head for the movement of worms in the lawn, I see a far greater variety: larger and more lovely phloxes, richer heleniums, more charming zinnias, a score of hybrids which the buttonholes of 1900 never knew.

Rain has fallen heavily; the petals of the erigeron daisies are like damp whiskers. The touch of rain brings a touch of autumn to the garden and the countryside. Now the yuccas are in bloom, and, looking at the tall, pure cream spires of bells, I am sure my fondness for them rises from the fact that a pair grew by the gateway of the house with the orchard. In the hot weather, as the flower-stem rose from the blue leaf-swords, there was a touch of claret-brown on the buds. Gradually as they opened they grew more and more cream, more and more pure. The flower-stems threw out branches, and the branches branchlets, until there were, perhaps, three hundred flowers blooming or just ready to bloom on the seven-foot stem. Each of these individual flowers is more than anything else like a Christmas rose, except that where the Christmas rose is pure and milky, rather austere and cold, the yucca-bell is pure and creamy and in effect like Chinese ivory. As the beads of fresh rain hang on them now the flowers look purer than ever, so very like ivory bells with six pure white clappers inside. The tall spire of these bells, of which there are probably two hundred in bloom at once, looks aloof, magnificent, im-personal: less like a stalk of flowers than a piece of flower-carving, even flower-architecture. As yuccas go, this is probably a small plant, yet it succeeds in giving a palatial impression. It rises above the rest of the August flowers, even the hollyhocks, like a temple of bells.

"That yucca looks lovely," says my gardener, "now that it's blowing." He uses the word as I should use "blooming," as Gilbert White used it and as Elizabethans used it. He uses it quite naturally. "That clematis is going to blow." To me this sounds very odd, because I use "blowing" to mean exactly the opposite of "blooming." I use it of a flower that is going over, that has bloomed and is now blown. "Blown roses on the grass." I use it in the sense of full-blown; so that for me August is the full-blown month. The year is full open and ripe and about to seed. With its yucca towers of bells, its hollyhocks and agapanthus, its exotic tall petunias and glowing regiments of dahlias, its burning zinnias and fuchsias, above all, perhaps, with its drowsy companies of butterflies tumbling all the hot day on the buddleia flowers, it is a month of blowing beauty.

XI

Wealden Beauty

The sunlight of August is strong on the fields of corn; by September it begins to fall more softly on the distances. You hear a robin begin to sing a little on a cool morning, but there are hot days to come. There is something painfully sweet and cold in this first sound of robin-song after the late summer silence. It is like the cooling down of the summer streams.

In late summer, before the war, I used to feel a deep nostalgia for new and sometimes distant horizons: France, Bavaria, the Austrian Tyrol; the high feather-clouded skies of Romney Marsh, the sea-shore, the country rolling down to the sea. When it was not possible to satisfy a distant dream, we used to satisfy a nearer one. There is a piece of country whose boundaries run slightly north-eastward from the sea at Rye, west of the Rother Levels, and up into the higher country east of Tunbridge Wells, and then due eastward to the North Downs about Godmersham and Wye, and then back through Tenterden, Appledore, and the Isle of Oxney. Roughly an isosceles triangle, with its southerly point in Sussex, touching the sea, this piece of country creates in me the restless impression that I have lived in it before. This feeling, though I was born and brought up a hundred and fifty miles away, becomes very strong in late August. It is a feeling of dreamy disquietude, a strong feeling that an experience out of the past remains unfinished and that now some new journey, a day by the sea, an hour or two on the wide marshlands, will bring it to completion. All this merely arises, perhaps, out of childhood memories, for as a child I often came southward with my parents to spend holidays mostly on the Sussex coast. We also went northward and eastward, but it was only in the South that we played the game of looking for the family name. Our family had long been noted for being fishermen, butterfly fiends, bird-lovers, naturalists; some members of it got their living from it, and it used to be said that wherever there was a wood or a river you would find a Bates; I was even proud that a Bates, though he had no connection with us, had written " A Naturalist and the Amazon." So our game used to be to search the narrow streets and the harbour quays of those Sussex towns for fishermen, boat-men, bird-stuffers, naturalists and even gardeners who bore our name. The number we found was astonishing; I remember once that we arrived at a boarding-house, went upstairs to our rooms and looked out of the window. And there on the opposite side of the street, as if he had known we were coming, a taxidermist had painted our name in large letters over his dingy shop. That delighted us, and still delights me. Twenty-five years later I still play the game of looking at shop-fronts for the names of these Bateses who, as my father used to say, got along quite well without hard work.

From these early experiences arises the feeling, perhaps, that this stretch of the South country is a second home. There are pieces of country—Wales is a notable example for me and, I believe, for many people—which create an instantaneous impression of unhappiness and gloom. You are no sooner in them than you long, with misery, to be out of them. They sour the spirit. There are towns—again the dour valley towns of Wales, the dourer town-villages of Scotland and even some much over-praised places of the West country—which create the same effect. But on me this triangle of Kent and Sussex has the friendly, tranquillizing effect of a familiar room. Whenever I leave it, going westward to what is supposedly the rich country of Devon, or northward to the flat, downright, half-industrialized Midlands, or even for some ambitious tour to the western lochs of Scotland, I come back to it with a renewed pleasure. The easy familiarity of it folds round me and I am glad to be home.

Easy and familiar—but also very varied and very beautiful. For this piece of country, from the wooded hollows that lie like giant birds' nests just behind the ridge of the North Downs as they run parallel to the Folkestone road to the view of Rye standing like a medieval fortified town above the Rother Levels, is the complete and generous English pastoral. It has a little of everything except mountains. It has downland and marsh, forest and heath, corn and hops, river and woodland, pond and pasture, churches and castles, ports and the sea. Its orchards are incomparable. It grows everything, from the primroses which are like moonlight on every roadside in spring, to the quinces which glow like the golden decorations of Christmas-trees in the Wealden gardens in autumn, with rich loveliness. Its little towns are

monuments to one of the only two industries—agriculture apart
—which have ever beautified the English township.   Cloth and
wool alone have left us a cultural and architectural legacy out of
industries long since dead, and towns like Cranbrook, Tenterden
and Hawkhurst are the legacies of cloth.   Of Tenterden it is
enough to say that it could sit with grace in the front row of any
prize-winning selection of English county towns.   That charming
High Street of black-and-white and tile-hung houses of warm
terra-cotta, widening to a sort of tree-lined boulevard at one end,
is hardly surpassed in England.   What Cranbrook lives on today
I don't know.   You get the impression of a town trying to
remember what once made it important—of people idling at street
corners, of shops always a little behind the times, an impression
of rosy-white charm a little dusted over and dominated from every
angle by a white windmill that towers above the town like a
giant toy.

This same impression of rosy-whiteness, mellowing in places to
plum-red and cream, broken in places by the sharp striping of
black and white, runs all through the villages, from Charing at
the foot of the great downland beech-woods on through the
Weald until the supreme expression of it is reached in Winchelsea
and Rye.   You might start from Charing, from the hill above
which there is a view that seems to take in half England, and by
going down through Smarden, Biddenden, Sissinghurst, Goudhurst, Benenden, Newenden, Northiam and Brede see a chain of
villages which are like a row of matched and graduated stones on
a necklace, warm and clean and fresh, not one out of place.   The
sharp half-timbering, magnificent at Biddenden, lights up the
landscape ; the warm-coloured tiles, clay-orange, yellow-russet,
pink-brown, tone it down.   The fashion of tile-hanging, of using
heart-shaped or tiles of some other shape to cover the house-sides,
gives many of these villages their distinguished character.   The

*The red and amber foolscaps of oast-
houses tipped as if with white feathers.*

impression created by even the best brick is bound to be flat. These tiles, hanging and overlapping, have something of the shadowy charm of window-shutters. They catch the falling light and hold it in a series of warm fancy parallels edged with shade. Lichen grows on them often in ringworms of lemon and green, so that sometimes a roof or a house-side seems to flower in the sun.

With two exceptions these villages are on the flat, tied sturdily to Wealden clay. Goudhurst and Brede are the notable exceptions, and from Goudhurst there is a view that destroys completely the notion that the Weald is merely a plain of mud and clay. From this steep village street, with its swan-pond, high-stepped houses and shining magnolias on the russet walls of tiles, the conception is of a country whose contours are literally flowering before the eyes. Fold after fold of orchard and wood, pasture and hop-garden run away into a distance limited by the heavy line of the Sussex Downs, a series of valleys splashed blue-green by the sprayed hops in summer, by the pink and white of the spring orchards, darkened by much holly and pine and chestnut, uplifted by the red and amber foolscaps of oast-houses tipped as if with white feathers. Sometimes, especially about the Goudhurst country, you can stand on one side of a valley and see very little except the slope of the other side, its hop-gardens and orchards painted in dark parallels down the slant, the red and white splashes of farmsteads breaking up the squares of the fields, the dark holly-hedges throwing up into shining relief the yellow strips of corn. No other country in England quite gives the impression, as this does, of being ready-made Van Gogh : the shining corn, the dark parallels of crops, the folded blue distances, the red and white houses. Do painters never come here? Sometimes as I drive through this country I stop and frame my hands against the summer valley-sides in despair because I work in words instead of paint. A whole world of landscape-painting, of the truest English pastoral, flowers uninterpreted here summer after summer.

The charm of all this country lies not simply in its richness, which is remarkable, but in its rich variations within a comparatively small space. Country composed almost solely of pasture and elm and hedgerow, as in the southern part of Leicestershire, seems to damp the mind. There is country of the same kind in Eastern Yorkshire and, indeed, in every part of the great eastern English plain. It is when country begins to fold into a series of quickly repeated valleys, and when soil and climate are so happily blended that you can grow not only standard crops like wheat and potatoes and grass, but specialized crops, with all the specialized design and architecture their culture entails, like hops and cherries, strawberries and Spanish chestnut, that landscape becomes a perfect delight. Softened by sun and sea-wind, such a district must become in time a sort of vast garden whose crop rotations are endless, a huge tract of fertile landscaping rich with more or less permanent touches of design—the woods, the orchards, the hop-gardens—that will go on delighting generation after generation. Its luxuriance is such that it overflows into the gardens. Great hydrangeas of blue and pink bloom by the houses, fuchsias spill down terraces of rock, quinces glow everywhere in the long, temperate autumns that, in good years, bring out the primroses in November. Not signs of the sub-tropical, of course, and not to be compared with the extreme West country, but touches of embroidery on a land already distinguished by the happy design given by great fertility.

All through this country the feeling of the nearness of the sea is pleasant. From the high points of the North Downs you can see the smoke-stacks of ships beyond Dungeness, but as you go over through the green switchback of the valleys between Charing and Rye there is scarcely another point, I think, at which you can get a glimpse of the sea. Yet to know that you are travelling down to the sea, even without a sight of it until the hills break abruptly above the marshes landward of Rye, creates a kind of mild stimulant pleasure in the mind. When finally you do see the sea, there is, I think, a slight feeling of disappointment. For here, about Rye and Winchelsea, the sea is in the wrong place. It is divorced from the true land, the cliff on which both Rye and Winchelsea stand, and lies rather meanly beyond a couple of miles of sea-marsh broken in one place by the mud-banked Rother, which still takes moderate ships, and farther west by the dark, lonely fortress of Camber Castle, isolated between the two towns and the sea. All this, of course, is the result of a great sea catastrophe. In the fourteenth century the sea advanced and took off this limb of land, destroying four-fifths of the port of Winchelsea in a night of natural calamity for which there is, I suppose, no parallel in our recent history. Winchelsea remains broken and enchanted, its one remaining church cut in half, the ghost of what might have been the most charming coastal town in England.

Rye remains. What to say of it after its years of arty re-discovery I hardly know. If there is a sea-town in England that is easier on the eyes, I have not yet found it. To say that everyone knows it, that those crazy cobbled streets of russet houses and exclusive numbers are now self-conscious pictures for the tourist is not enough. In England the beautiful town, or the town in the beautiful situation, is faced with two choices: the terrors of the tea-and-ham-and-eggs shack, with all the traps for tourists which have desolated the gorge at Cheddar and the long glen at Matlock, or the hand of middle-class preservation. In spite of art and snobbery, there is no doubt which is the better choice, and to this Rye has long since been comfortably given up. Useless to protest that it is full of tea-shops. Naturally it is. Equally useless to protest that it exists solely for the pleasure of middle-class ladies, arty artists and cliques of writers. The port still has its trade ; ships still come up the yellow-grey Rother estuary ; they make fish-nets here by the ton, and the town has a life of its own.

As you come back into Kent across the Rother Levels, where the skyscapes above the flat dyke-lands are vast and snowy with sea-cloud and the reeds flower fawn-silver by the waterside and the great hedges of hawthorn, you see the land rising again in the north towards the Isle of Oxney and Appledore. The true marsh lies farther east, full of that odd air of remote beauty which sea always gives to sea-marshes and which has something to do with the larger and loftier area of sky that can be seen on flat land. The villages are small here, without the luxuriance of the upland villages of the Weald ; the churches are squat, often flint-faced. But there is a church here that is pleasure even to a man who has been brought up, as I was, on the cream of church architecture, the glorious diet of Midland battlement and spire. Brookland should not be missed : simple, primitive, cold as marsh air, its windows of clear glass, its font solid lead, and the great wooden bell-tower completely detached from the church itself. They say that smugglers were once active in and about this stout, plain-windowed little church, and I don't doubt it at all.

At Appledore you are among the charm again : the russet and brown, pink and white houses, the neat air of reflected prosperity. A windmill or two uplifts the already high ridge ; there are long views towards the sea, then heavy woodlands that cut them off. There was a port here once, before the abruptly changed course of the Rother, in 1287, finished Appledore's days of sea pros-perity. Now there is no touch of the sea ; only pastoral calm, deep primrose woodland, road-dykes mauve with lady-smock in April, dark ponds lit up all summer by yellow water-lilies. And here, perhaps, is the place to say something about the roads of this piece of country. If there is anything crazier than this jumble of lanes that wriggle and tangle together like eels on their way to the coast, I have not yet found it in England. It used to be a fairly regular custom of mine to drive round and about here on Sunday evenings in summer. In all these excursions I think I never navigated a course that could be called conscious or without getting hopelessly lost only five or ten miles from home. If these roads were designed to fuddle invaders or, which is most improbable, to help smugglers, then they were successfully made. There are no roads quite so irritating and charming in the whole of England.

But however you get lost on these roads there is always an unfailing compass-point; it can be seen from almost everywhere in this flatter land—the straight back of the North Downs and the great bearskin of woodland, almost black in winter and summer, fiery-bronze in autumn, that lies above the sun-bleached loins of chalk. As the sea attracts you to the south, so this line of hills has some sort of magnetism as you turn north. And as you come up off the yellow clay, crowded with skylarks in spring, and up the first step of the richer cherry-lands that lie on the ledge between Weald and hills and so into sight of the stark chalk that suddenly breaks into beech-woods of superb height on the hill-tops, the feeling of attraction grows stronger still. To know what lies on the other side of the hill—this feeling inevitably draws you up the deep-carved lanes along which the summer flowers grow richer as the soil grows poorer and whiter, up to the rising wall of beeches and the eternal copper floor of leaves swept by dark yews. The depth of silence here on hot summer days, when there is no wind and the chalk is blinding on the eyes and the rock-roses are brilliant lemon in the sun, can be immense, the feeling of isolation splendid. And on days when the warm sea-strong air blows up from the valley and the sun is very bright the whole of that flat, green view below seems sometimes to tilt and rock in the drowsy, exhilarating windiness of the air.

To climb the hill through the beeches and to see what finally does lie behind is a piece of the pleasantest discovery. It would be reasonable to expect the land to flatten out, as, in fact, it does only a mile or two farther northward, but here it breaks into a succession of steep valleys, almost pits, falling and rising grandly, flanked and topped with woodlands, furrowed by small lanes driven deeply through the chalk. If the Weald is an excellent example of man-made, man-beautified countryside, of which the greater part of the charm arises from the orchards, the woods and the architecture, these downland hollows are a good example of what you might call natural country, in which a country like England is inevitably poor. This is the sort of country, so rich in natural contour and so much more enriched by woods that are like slices of forgotten forest, which we cry out to have preserved, but which in a way successfully preserves itself. For there is little man can do with these steep chalk slopes; the farmsteads here seem small, there are no orchards, no hops; you see sometimes a small strip of cornland, a few chickens, a little meadow of hay. But the land is, for once, stronger than the people on it. It stands above and outside the main stream of cultivation: strong and decorative, barren but rich, useless but remarkably lovely.

It is a striking fact that the villages here are poor, and as you get farther and farther east, far outside my chosen triangle, poorer still. There is once more a charming russetness about Charing and Wye and, again far out of the triangle, a superb black and white village square at Chilham. For the rest, there is no Wealden richness—for the simple reason that there was in the past no Wealden prosperity, no cloth, no rich merchants to leave out of industry a legacy of enchanting culture. It is only rarely, most notably in the Cotswolds and Suffolk, that you find that happy state of things. And perhaps it is asking too much. For it is fairly certain that if these downland hollows, rich with cowslips and bluebells and rarer orchids in spring and summer, always superb with their rolling woodlands, had been graced with towns and villages as architecturally fine as Biddenden, Smarden, Benenden, Appledore, Goudhurst and Tenterden, this break in the long ridge of north downland would have been one of the tourist spots of England. Even as it is it stands with West Sussex, parts of Hampshire and even the much-praised over-ripe valleys of Devonshire, as country unsurpassed of its kind. Indeed, if there is more beautifully varied country—as I recall the Lakes, the New Forest, the valleys of Exe and the Dove, I am aware that there is a powerful category of more impressive country—than that contained in this small triangle, whose sides are not longer than twenty miles if you take the straight line, then I shall hope to see it when petrol is no longer something you buy with a coupon and nurse like Napoleon brandy.

XII

The Strangeness of Fish

At intervals during the summer we have been fishing together: the sergeant, the corporal, the private and myself. "If it wasn't for the fishing we should all go bloody crazy," the sergeant says. He looks tired and thoughtful and will be glad when the war is over; he has several children. The corporal is young and fresh and very pleasant; a nice fellow. The private is one of those soft-mannered Cockneys, open, easy, extraordinarily polite, extraordinarily intelligent, who seem more like countrymen than Londoners. In peace-time all fish in the Thames; all have a certain feeling for the country, perhaps because they are anglers and because any piece of water is a piece of country, that is surprising to me. More and more, as the summer goes on, they seem to become part of the country. You hear them talk with nostalgia of days on the Thames, when the bream and the barbel were rising strong below the weirs; and there is no doubt they will one day talk with nostalgia of this Kentish lake, where the tench and pike seemed to walk on the lily-leaves on hot summer evenings and the kingfishers were like blue storm-sparks in the dark summer rain.

Every week I am asked by someone what the country will be like after the war; and every time I am asked I think of the sergeant, the corporal and the private; of the thousands of men like them in all parts of the country; of the evacuees; of the children transplanted from towns. And thinking of them, and looking at the same time at the country, I am forced to the conclusion that after the war there will be little or no change in the country itself—that is, in the face of the country and even, perhaps, in the habits of the country—but only in the attitude of people towards the country. From this attitude, if it is strong enough, some change may arise. For it must be remembered that the great changes in the countryside during almost the last two hundred years have come from outside the country, made by events which, being mechanical, scientific, educational or merely profit-making, appeared to have no direct relationship to rural life. The steam-engine, the railway system and the internal combustion engine, though they were designed to have no particular part in rural life, all caused revolutions within it. The enclosures of the late eighteenth and early nineteenth century were economic in purpose, but their social and moral consequences were enormous. The war of 1914-1918 was fought entirely on foreign soil, yet its effect on the conduct of English rural life was shattering. The high explosives of 1941 have so far shown no sign of being more devastating socially than the events which in

The sergeant, the cor-
poral and the private.

1914-1918 shattered Church and squirearchy to bits, and there appears to be no set of rules to explain why a violent conduct in one part of the world, for clearly stated purposes like freedom and democracy, should produce entirely illogical reactions in another. A soldier who fought under blistering Arabian sun, as part of the Arab revolt, might have been very surprised to find that the post-war change which mattered most to him was not whether Arabs were happier or more civilized, but the fact that in the villages of England the parson had lost all, or most, of his power. It may be part of the futility of wars that a man appears to fight for one thing and succeeds only in getting something entirely different. In 1914 no slogans appeared to urge a fight for the smashing of the squirearchy, the undermining of the Church, or the creation of a larger middle class; yet these were among the most positive results of the conflict. If the war had been openly designed for these purposes, it is highly probable, of course, that it would never have been fought.

So whenever I see the sergeant gazing moodily at his float, and whenever he looks up to ask me, "What do you think of this bloody war?" I think of this. For the sergeant has a right to be moody. He is a soldier; a soldier is trained to fight battles; and it may well seem to him wrong that for a large part of the time he is watching the quivering of a float on a piece of water so peaceful and untouched by the life of today that it might not have changed for two hundred and fifty years. He has a right to be thoughtful. For as a man with several children it is clear that the war will affect him profoundly. It has, in fact, begun to affect him profoundly already; he is no longer a townsman; his wife and children live in the country, forced there by one of the largest social revolutions—the evacuation of cities—of modern times. After the war, perhaps—who can tell?—he may cease to be a townsman altogether. There may be implanted in the

minds of his children the idea that city life, if only because it can
be destroyed in a split second by a bomb, is intolerable. He may
find himself a small-holder, with the land about him nationalized.
He may find himself part of a revolution which was never men-
tioned in the original programme of war. Like thousands of
others, he may wake one day to the surprising reflection that
massacre in Warsaw, bloodshed in the Ukraine, heat and thirst
in Libya, attack and counter-attack in Greece, have produced a
totally unpredicted change in the manner of his life.

All these reflections are vague, speculatory, perhaps absurd.
But whenever I am asked if there will be change in the English
countryside after the war, and more still when I read the categorical
post-war programmes put out grandiosely by politicians, I begin
to think this way. One speculation about the future is as good
as another; as good and, of course, as pointless. The sergeant,
who stands for perhaps a million of his kind, is worried; life
is disrupted; he cannot, as he often says to me, see the bloody
end of it all. It perhaps does not occur to him that there is no
end, that life is not a straight line with convenient barriers to
mark each era of conflict, peace or disruption. He will never see
the end of it all.

Yet there are things of which he can be quite certain. As he
walks through the park which is his barracks and down past the
chestnut copse to the lake where the poplars will begin to turn
soon to lemon-yellow in the late autumn sun, he must be struck
sooner or later by the fact that, whatever else happens, this lake,
these trees and the life in them and about them will not change.
Cities and lives have been changed; people sleep in the bowels of
the earth; men fly and fight at a fantastic height above the earth.
Yet perhaps the most striking thing about war is its ultimate lack
of effect on Nature. The seasons come and go with a magnificent
indifference. And the sergeant, who shakes his head and sighs

sometimes and says as he looks across the water, "Never know there was a bloody war on, would you?" is simply expressing that profoundly true and comforting fact. It is probably that fact, indeed, expressed for him in the unaccountable and fascinating lives of the fish for which he so impatiently and moodily angles, which keeps him from going crazy.

The habits of fish are certainly unaccountable. There are many things we do not know about birds. It is only a few years since the great mysteries of the cuckoo and the eel were cleared up. Bird-watching is a pastime of thousands of people, ranging from children to prime ministers; it is responsible for hundreds of books a year, thousands of articles; in the pursuit of it ornithologists spend months on lonely islands, years in research. It is very much of a modern phenomenon. What has been called the marriage of classification and observation—consummated on the marriage-bed of the theory of organic evolution in the nineteenth century—has, perhaps, been largely responsible for it. But birds can be seen; they are beautifully coloured; they sing; their habits are delightful; the reproduction of their species is undoubtedly accompanied by the most charming accessory beauty—i.e., eggs, nest and song—in the whole of Nature. No wonder birds are so much loved. But fish do not sing; they cannot easily be seen; they are very beautiful in motion and colour, but their reproduction has little enchantment, and out of their element they lose all attraction. Seeking for a standard of human comparison, we are forced to compare them, not with ships, the most beautiful vehicles devised by man, but with submarines, the most detestable. Even here birds have the advantage. In all flight, whether by bird, man or insect, there is great visual appeal; it will always be regarded, I think, as a miracle of mechanics and beauty.

So birds are naturally the most loved of all wild animals; they play, perhaps, the largest economic, scientific and æsthetic part in our lives. Fish are mysterious and attractive, but not, I think, much loved; they play an æsthetic part in the lives of a few, but never a great proportion of, people; the spawning of perch among the spring reeds, for example, is probably seen every year by a handful of fishermen; but the first call of the cuckoo is heard, and awaited, by millions. We seem also to marvel at exactly opposite manifestations in fish and birds. In fish, for example, we marvel at weight; in birds at the lack of it. The more a fish weighs, the more remarkable it seems. But the lightness of birds, especially small birds, is a wonder. Even a heron, which may be three feet in length and have a wing-span of five or six feet, weighs only three pounds. This is, however, a great weight for a bird. A snipe, which is a game-bird, weighs, for example, only four ounces; a sparrow-hawk only five or six. A wood-pigeon weighs only about twenty ounces, a moor-hen sixteen. When we come to really small birds, the weights become astonishing. A nightingale weighs six drachms, a blue-tit under half an ounce, a wren two and three-quarter drachms. Perhaps surprisingly a swift weighs nearly an ounce, and a cuckoo, not surprisingly to anyone who has seen a young cuckoo being fed, a little over a quarter of a pound. A yellow-hammer weighs seven drachms, a grey wagtail five drachms, a corn-bunting about two ounces. But perhaps a tree-creeper, which looks so like a minute mouse as it fidgets swiftly on the bark, has the record: it weighs only two drachms.

We reckon a catch of fish in pounds, stones, hundredweights. But it has been computed that, if all the bird population of this country in May-time were killed for food, each member of the population would get half an ounce, or just under, of meat. We sometimes overlook the wonder of very obvious things. So perhaps we, too, often overlook the fact that in a world where power and size are reckoned as of supreme importance, and where the element of destruction has wider and wider influence every day, a tiny creature like the tree-creeper, which is just large enough to come within the range of human persecution, should survive and flourish successfully.

Skilled observation of birds is not easy; but observation of fish in their natural element is, of course, almost impossible. It is, perhaps, surprising that fishermen know as much about fish as they do. Yet how much do they know? A bird is hatched, grows, comes to full size within a short time and remains there. A fish goes on growing, from a two-eyed mote flickering in the spring water to a creature of ten, twenty, forty pounds, apparently indefinitely, with the result that there are more legends than facts about fish. There are legends of monster pike and tench; no fact proves or disproves them. In habits fish remain, as they have done for all time, highly mysterious and perplexing. There is the legend that they feed after rain; another that they are sluggish and dull and satiated in very hot weather. Time after time, in rain and after rain, I have angled without catching a fish; yet recently, in temperatures of ninety degrees, I caught fish with that absurd ease and regularity that gives every fisherman such false confidence in his powers. It is reputed to be necessary to angle for tench on the very bottom of the stream; yet I frequently catch them at the top. Late evening and very early morning is the hard rule for tench; yet I have caught them about noon and in the late afternoon. Pike feed, you will be told, on sharp, cold, windy days, with a touch of ice or storm, hardly ever on soft, sluggish, westerly days. But give me the warm days, from my experience, and not the cold. You perhaps know that a certain bird feeds on insects, seeds, fruit, and that it feeds a great deal; yet there is simply no knowing how certain fish will feed, at what depth of water, at what time of day, on what and for how long. There are anglers who claim an instinct about these things;

others who act on experience and the few known facts. Their combined perspicacity is very small beside the incalculable and apparently capricious behaviour of the fish. If I turn up a modern book on angling, for example, it will tell me little more than the quaint Daniel's "Rural Sports," a hundred and fifty years old, the angling literature of the eighteenth century, or Walton. Yet if I turn up a modern book on birds it will seem revolutionary, perhaps incredibly so, beside the books of a hundred and even fifty years ago. So much begins to be known and discovered about birds that it is necessary, and has been necessary for some long time, to deal with species separately. The amount of bird-literature becomes colossal. Yet much of the literature about fish is trivial, reactionary, sentimental. It appears to me that less has been done for fish—I exclude now, of course, deep-sea researches and experiments, such as those of Dr. Beebe—than for ants and bees. So as anglers we continue to behave largely with absurd seriousness and ignorance, perfecting manual skill and yet knowing very little about the fish we try so patiently to catch.

And perhaps this is what the sergeant means when, as we sit together under the alder-trees and it is cool after a hot spell and the water is dark-coloured and still and full of promise and yet the fish are not biting, he suddenly bursts out: "It's a bloody mystery." But I can never be quite sure; for he may be thinking simply of the war, the paradox that sees him so often fighting for freedom with a fishing-rod, or just mankind in general. The description would fit them all.

131

XIII

The Parish Pump

The August rain is heavy and dark; it seems to blacken the green of the trees and wash out the burnished shine on the wheat. At the same time it gives the oats a fresh, airy grace. Beads of clear rain hang on the beards. The black seeds are shown up like darts. The oat-stalks are washed clean, opalescent, and all through the rainy, windless days they do not move. For some days the wheat has an astonishing colour, especially against the hedgerows. It is part green, part gold, partly the colour of dark honey. The colours shade into each other and are more than ever like waves as the wind gently blows the corn.

In beans and corn the poppies are now almost over. They hang like damp, scarlet rags, and thistles, mauve and savage, bloom in their place. There has been little of what you could call hoeing all summer; so the wheat is tangled with pink convolvulus and thistle and white camomile, and even willow-herb rises pink now along the hedge-sides, where meadow-sweet is like frothed cream among the green blackberries and the straw-coloured late honey-suckle and the milky-green nuts of the hazels. Beyond the hedgerows, on roadsides, grasses have been burnt blonde by weeks of sun and are the new platinum colour of hair, bleached and shining; but below the blonde stalks the new grass is growing, as it is also growing in the meadows, in a flush of emerald. In the meadows also there is a new flower. Where the flax was laid on the grass for its spring retting, broad lines of flax-stalk have come up and are now in bloom, in bands of pale blue that run across the fields. If by some chance the flax should seed and spread again, it is possible that we may have blue meadows in late summer that will be comparable in loveliness to the golden and white meadows of late spring. But now, apart from the delicate blue streams of flax, almost the only flower that strikingly lights up the August meadow is yarrow, once dead white, but now stained to crushed strawberry by weeks of sun.

But on roadsides, on the edges of corn, in corn and along field tracks everywhere there is now in bloom the loveliest of late summer flowers. Pale mauve scabious rise everywhere in the blonde grass and the honey-brown corn. The distinguished round heads, neat and soft as the bronzy-scarlet pincushions of the wild roses, look cool and dignified. There is a gentle, tickling scent from them as you stoop down and touch the cream-flecked heads that vary a little in colour, from very pale mauve through flushed lilac to strong half-purple, and on hot afternoons there is always a sleepy rise of meadow-brown butterflies and occasional blues, which flitter up from the flowers and hover and settle again, drowsily closing wings that seem to look at you with a steady

133

dark-brown eye. You will find that scabious become more plentiful and, if possible, more beautiful as you get to higher land, and I remember once walking in the Cotswold Hills in late summer and seeing all along the broad roadsides, by the sheep-grey stone walls, great stretches of scabious, which were only matched by the great stretches of harebell and yellow rock-rose and occasional bursts of deep purple trumpets of Campanula patula that were almost as dark and fine as clustered gentians. Everywhere along the hot, stony Cotswold roadsides these mauve flowers were cool on the eyes. There were tall mauve nettle-leaved campanulas, too, like slim, wild Canterbury bells, and occasional breaks of pink rest-harrow. Beside the china hairbells the dark patula were almost exotic, and sometimes there was a strain in the scabious of pure lilac, deepening to pink, or another strain, darker, deepening to purple. It was fascinating to see this separation of colour, so that scarcely two flowers were alike. There was knapweed too, now I remember, that sometimes showed these variations, though never so strongly. The flowers, too, are always coarser, harsher, lacking the delicacy of the scabious, even when they sometimes break to pure white, as I have seen them do.

I do not remember a summer when grass grew so tall or was bleached so white by sun. The roadsides looked as if covered with thin, shaggy oats. The village green, the Forstal, looked until yesterday much the same, but yesterday, at last, tractor and mower arrived, and the grass in two and a half hours was laid down in fawn-green swathes. More than half its value as hay has gone, but it will be carried for stack-topping and will earn its cost. I am glad to see it down, partly because dead grass is a depressing sight in mid-winter, partly because as chairman of the parish council I must do my best, somehow, to see that it gets cut and carried away. The fact of being chairman of the parish

Meadow-brown butterflies and occasional blues, which
flitter up from the flowers and hover and settle again.

council is always, to some people, a funny thing. It is one of the English country jokes; it belongs to the category of old chestnuts which still go off with a dusty pop—mothers-in-law, babies' napkins, the husband taking off his shoes at the foot of the stairs, income-tax, sergeant-majors and the rest; the English parish council has a fairly honourable place. On the long chain of democracy, which we refurbish with such vigour every twenty years or so, it hangs like a clumsy and antiquated bead which no one remembers to shine. Its proceedings have been so often burlesqued, its chairmen so often guyed, that probably many people think of it, when they think of it at all, in terms of music-hall or comic broadcast: as something so dead and ineffectual in reality that it must be made fun of to be kept alive at all. Yet this same chestnut is part of English democracy. It is the country parliament. As long as its functions continue the English rural labourer can get up on his feet and spout his piece and elect his local government. The moment it becomes extinct these privileges, and perhaps the rural labourer with them, become extinct also.

When I recently took the chair at the meeting of my parish council it was something like my twentieth meeting, and my fifth or sixth of the war. For two hours we discussed what I suppose were trivialities and what I suspect the rest of the village concluded would be trivialities, since only one person out of a population of two hundred and fifty was present. Reflecting on this, I began to wonder if the functions of the English parish council system are really becoming archaic and in consequence comic, or if this was just another sample of country indifference, of the kind stigmatized with "the more you do for them, the more you may."

It is true that country people are notoriously indifferent to the system by which they are governed; but those who govern them are often indifferent also, though with a kind of indifference that is sometimes a betrayal of public trust. For instance, if I look back over the records of the parish council of my own village, I find again and again this entry: "At the meeting of the parish council held on such-and-such a date (date often wrong) no business was conducted, there being an insufficient number of councillors present." On the occasion when business was conducted, it is apparent that it was often of a footling kind; the dreary minutes are dead, written with clumsy and colourless formality. Payments of expenses are noted and approved; but long later it becomes apparent that they, too, are muddled. The clerk makes payments out of his own pocket, content to reimburse himself at some future time. No one bothers. It is pretty clear that for years no one cared, that many people were shoved into office and remained there, bored, ineffectual, inarticulate and perhaps not even knowing why they were there until they were shoved out again.

This is one period. Take another: the chairman is now a man of both ideas and background, though unfortunately both are mistaken. He is a genial, conservative, slightly pompous man who wishes to infuse these qualities, together with some town ideas of improvement and "pep," into the government of the village; he is a townsman who, knowing nothing of country values, wishes to see himself in the position of country squire. He has read somewhere, perhaps, that village folk need a lead, that they never do anything unless shown a glowing outside example. So his method of government is that of the feudal squire: I want it done my way, and it will be done. Unfortunately, it is getting on towards the middle of the twentieth century, the feudal squire is a victim, like the Church, of the great revolution of 1914-1918, and even in tiny villages there is bound to be someone who, sooner or later, resents the rule of autocracy. So he is ousted, and I confess I do my part in ousting him. But not before he has cut down a hundred magnificent trees, which include beautiful specimens of acacia and African oak, and has landed the village with a financial debt, together with a debt of bitterness, which can never be redeemed.

So the system of muddled indifference and the system of vigorous but mistaken autocracy have both been tried. The only difference in their respective failures is that the one has negative and erasable results, and that the other has results of a positive indelible stupidity. Of the two, I prefer the rule of indifference.

Yet both are wrong. Villages cannot, or at least should not, be run this way: by a combination of carelessness and somnolent indifference to what can be and ought to be done, or a combination of grandiose ideas and a serious misconception of everything fundamental to rural life. Yet they are run like this in England today; and they are run, too, on the equally questionable combinations of bigotry and jealousy, pecksniffing and backbiting, bureaucratic jiggery-pokery and plain, dumb slackness of heart.

When I found myself voted chairman of my own parish council, with a council composed entirely of working men (one gardener, one estate hand, two skilled workers), I knew that, as far as experience went, I had no qualifications. Yet I felt I could not go wrong if I acted with scrupulous fairness, with at least an attempt at judicial balance in disputes, and without bias; or if I gave every man not only the right to speak, but to speak plainly; or if I encouraged rather than damped down intelligence, individuality and the inquisitive ferreting that the country mind loves; or if I created a feeling of informality, equality and no nonsense; above all, if I did not impose my own ideas, individuality and prejudices rigidly and with superiority, thus creating the very thing—class consciousness—I hate most in contact with my fellow-men.

And now, after four years, I think this has worked well. Knowing the folly of trying to force the country mind towards decision and change, I have rarely attempted to force a proposal or a scheme. Nothing has ever been cut and dried. I was, and am, quite disinterested; I did not, and still do not, care any more for the rights of one man's property than another's. As a council we were fortunate in two things: nobody on the council was employed by the chairman, nor was the clerk to be got at. So fear of outspokenness was ruled out; fear of consequences was ruled out. The clerk himself was an outsider, a man trained in rural district affairs, and in many ways excellent. Taking him back to the town in my car after the meetings I could sometimes reflect sadly with him on the question of country bigotry, vindictiveness, slackness, suspicion, ingratitude, the too-prevalent creed of always wanting something out of something, and if possible for nothing.

Yet it was not really these things which bothered us. What bothered us was the long legacy of past councils: the years of inefficiency, unattended meetings, indifference as to whether trees were cut down or common land privately appropriated. For three years we fought through an amazing jungle of legalities, dishonest dealing and weary argument in order to retrieve for public ownership a five-acre common that had somehow passed into private hands. Past councils had watched such shady dealing with open eyes. We disentangled the bungled affairs of centuries-old charities, the documents for which had often been lost. We fought against the closing of the village school, against rats, cases of bad sanitation, the long-windedness of rural councils. We fought against the deep-crusted, impervious, class-ridden autocracy of clerics whose contribution to village life could be measured only by the visiting bicycle (on fine afternoons and to the right people), the doffed hat and the frog-cold smile. We fought for council houses, safer corners, bus shelters, cleaner ditches and streets. We fought whenever we could and for whatever seemed worth fighting for.

And with what result? To hear again and again the rural parrot-cry: "The parish council never does anything."

Yet in twenty-odd meetings, when better housing conditions, important principles of common rights and child education were being discussed, the average public attendance has been less than one per meeting.

And who attended? The landowners, the farmers, the men who are the economic life of the area? Not once. The parson? No. The maiden ladies to whom property, legal rights and the petty privacy of the garden fence are parts of a jealously defended ritual? Never.

Yet these are the people of education, social background, economic independence, spare time. These are the people who should care. Is the country, in which they have chosen to live and do business, of no account to them at all? A lady says, "I love law; I love stocks and shares," and in that brief remark one sees reflected a whole life of selfish interests, a fanatical regard for profit and property, a deeply insulated indifference to all life except her own. A landowner worth a quarter of a million pounds shudders dying in an icy bedroom and barks at the nurse: "Bah! Who wants a fire? I can't afford such luxuries!" A rich country business man tells with delight of swindling an antique dealer out of a table worth fifty pounds more than is paid. A woman of independent means employs a gardener who is called up for the Army; he leaves on Thursday. The occasion to him is one of upheaval, sadness, apprehension, a certain bitterness at leaving wife and baby. But to the employer? An occasion only to argue whether or not she shall pay the week's full wages (two pounds) or dock for a day and a half. In such lives one is confronted with a selfishness beside which the Himalayas are a range of mole-hills.

To all these people, as to the section of the community known as "the villagers," the parish council is a common heritage. It is a tiny working fragment of the democratic machine. It is a symbol of free social expression, small but significant; it is a part of the larger privilege by which democratic man elects or ejects his government.

Has this any possible interest or significance for the outside world? I fancy it has. Sometimes the examination of the small thing may lead to a better understanding of the larger. In the present attitude of indifference towards the English parish council, both of electors and elected, there exists a great danger. It is a danger that must always beset democracy: the danger of taking privilege as a natural right. In this stagnant rural apathy, exemplified in hundreds of villages up and down England, may be seen the workings of the same dry-rot that contributed to the fall of France and may still, even after victory, bring the roof of English democracy tottering about our ears.

Thinking of it, I think also of some words of an ancestor of mine who got most of his education behind the plough. "You must make them suffer before you can make them understand."

XIV

Flowers and Downland

On a day in late summer all the beauty of summer rises like cream to the hills. The clouds come riding in from the sea. They are very white, but the waves of shadow unfolding across the white stubbles move with dark splendour, and in the wide blue intervals the sun is very hot under the wall of beeches. All across the open slope of downland the late flowers are in their glory. Where the beeches end there begins a narrow thicket of dogwood and wild clematis and spindle and blackberry, and where the thicket ends there begins a steep run of pink and mauve and yellow that ends only far down the slope, at the edge of the summer-bleached arable land. The wild clematis is in flower in lacy cream wreaths everywhere; the spindle-berries are already touched with rose ; the dewberries are black and luscious as they trail on the ground where the last small wild strawberries glow very scarlet among the flowers. There are a few wild raspberries and in one place, looking like strings of red bryony, a tree of wild red currant, dark scarlet, shining, untouched by birds. Soon there will be nothing but a glow of berry and leaf and seed all along the down ; but now, in late summer, not quite autumn, all the glory is in the flowers, and on hot afternoons, when even the wind is warm, in the drowsy crowds of butterflies that float everywhere like wind-shaken petals of scarlet and white and blue and coffee-brown.

There are two flowers now that shine out above all the rest. Pink bay willow-herb is thick and tall as corn, and underneath it, and between it, wild marjoram foams everywhere into purple-grey, pink-purple, grey-white flower. There is scarcely a foot of the higher down where they have not seeded and blossomed, so that it seems from a distant glance as if nothing else has survived the thick foam of pink that lies on the hill-side like an arrested flower-wave. For loveliness there is nothing to choose between them. They are very common; one lights up the air and the other the earth, and it is only when you look up their classic origins that you see how beautifully and aptly one was named. The Greeks, who had the words for so many things, had the words for marjoram. For its classic name is Origanum vulgare : from " oros," a hill, and " ganos," brightness—brightness to hilly places.

It is only when you begin to walk across the down that you find that the willow-herb and marjoram often give way, and in places quite deeply, to other flowers. It is a little too high for scabious, and there are flowers which never leave the thicket of dogwood and blackberry by the edge of the beeches. Nettle-leaved campanulas, like wands of mauve bells, are never far from the small thick trees. They are never out among the willow-herb, in the same way as the willow-herb never comes in to the shelter and support of the thicket, where red bryony hangs trails of un-shining crimson beads among the creamy clematis flowers and the purple-orange darts of bitter-sweet. These also are never far from the shadow and support of the thicket. But out in the open, on the thin chalk, there are flowers which, like marjoram and willow-herb, revel in the scorched open spaces. Bright lemon, with touches of bee-orange, the wild yellow snapdragons make vivid rings among the strawberry leaves, and groups of St. John's wort smother the scattered branches of dead larch with yellow single roses. Wild mignonette makes big creamy-lemon bushes that flower for a long time and that now, in late summer, are stalked with apricot pods of seed. Sometimes there is a bright blue bush of wild anchusa and another, deep frosty lilac, of wild valerian. The little brilliant yellow rock-roses, the expression of mid-summer, very clear and pure, have almost gone, and the tender blue milkworts with them. All the flowers now are stronger, heavier, more luscious, even coarse. The clumps of stunted ragwort have no delicacy; the dark bushes of deadly nightshade, with their sinister grey-purple bells and luscious black poison-cherries, seem artificial, like plants fashioned out of wood and iron, stiff and graceless, strangely unreal.

There are late summer flowers which you miss here: blue chicory, pink rest-harrow. Others, like purple knapweed, which is also sometimes white, outclimb the valley flowers and are here as thick as ever among the marjoram and the willow-herb. And on hot days, when the silence is deepened by the high monotone of big green grasshoppers, the butterflies themselves float drowsily everywhere like scraps of flower: flickering white Cabbages, plum-wine Peacocks, Common-Blues, Meadow Browns, Red Admirals, Tortoiseshells, Marbled Whites, big charming auburn fritillaries.

In their powdery and drowsy beauty they are very much part of summer's end, of the rich pink stretches of marjoram and willow-herb, the hot smell of blackberries ripening, the sea-foam clouds riding in over the green, tranquil, cornless land.

And as I sit looking over this pink stretch of down, below which the land is laid out with a kind of remote neatness, I am struck by the fact that its beauty is part of a fairly recent act of desolation. Wherever the willow-herb and the marjoram and the wild strawberries stretch there was only a few years ago a larch wood that was like a wood of lamp-posts. Until it was cut down there was no view to the sea. It was dark and flowerless; in spring the trees were feathered with leaves like summer asparagus, and in summer there were no strawberries and the shade was cold. The wood, when it was cut down, was cut down badly. Timber-tractors churned in across the soft chalk, making deep tracks, hauling away the larch-trunks but leaving every twig and tree-head that was without commercial value. I have since seen woods where bombs have fallen, and this was the same effect. As you looked at the scarred land, treeless now, choked with fallen larch-boughs, raw and desolate, you swore at the timber merchants because they did not know their business and because for years now the line and beauty of the hills would be killed by this strip of scorched and barren earth. You could not have guessed, just as you could not now guess that its pink and cloudy serenity is only thirty miles from the outposts of Calais, that soon, in a year or two, it would be a paradise of wild berry and butterfly and flower, from the bright, sharp days of March, when the violets spread like pools of deep purple and snowdrop white and grey across the chalk, on to October, when the dying beeches and spindles and dogwoods are themselves like giant flowers that reflect for the last time all the colours of summer and spring.

So this one rather careless act of what seemed like vandalism

145

has caused more change and more beauty on this stretch of hill-side than it has seen, perhaps, in fifty years and several wars. As I stand on it, in autumn, and look southwards, I am struck again, for perhaps the hundredth time, by the fact that wars depend a good deal on Nature, but that Nature seems not only independent of, but magnificently indifferent to, wars. Out above the coast, in the tranquil September sky, a plane flies beyond the steel masts of the radio station that are like grey match-sticks in the slightly misty air. I know where these masts are : the land is flat and bare ; the many dykes are fringed with deer-brown reed and purple loosestrife and soft grey wild hollyhocks. The skyscapes are wide and luminous with sea-light. Soon the plane disappears, and soon in its place there rises a black cloud of smoke that hangs and thickens over the sea. Something has happened ; the plane has gone ; the war has touched for a moment, with a distant and unexplained smudge, the calm beauty of a late September day that does not belong to one war or another, nor to one century or another, but to all time. In a little while the smoke thins and then vanishes altogether. The radio masts are clear and toy-like again down on the hazy coast. A train puffs among the woods, appearing and reappearing, and makes its way across what seems to be a deserted land. Something has happened and yet nothing has happened. A cataclysm shakes the world and yet the world goes on.

Soon the hot, still days of September seem very far away ; the rooks come away from the stubbles and break the evenings with great gabbles of alarm in the yellow-green elms, and there is a continuous commotion among the poplars : a flat clapping of thousands of paper hands. There is now an autumnal stirring of life that seems more like spring, and birds are back again in the seeding gardens.

For many weeks the blackbirds, freed from the great cherry

And now that the berberis are finished
they have turned to the elderberries.

orchards that surround us here, have been attacking the first berries with secret greed. They have a way of hiding among the blue fruits and leaves of the earlier berried berberis and then suddenly losing balance and flopping guiltily out, orange bills stained purple as a child's lips with blackberries. And now that the berberis are finished they have turned to the elderberries, performing the same guilty flopping, stripping the berry-stalks so clean that they are left like the red skeletons of little hands, or, after heavy rain, like fronds of claret seaweed. So gradually the rich, black feast of elders is lessening, and now there are fewer blackbirds than a month ago, and already for every blackbird there seems to be a dozen blue-tits, and for every tit there must be a million seeds.

After the brilliant raid of Red Admirals, Tortoise-shells, Peacocks and Painted Ladies on the lilac-branched buddleias in August and September there is nothing in the later country year which in beauty equals this autumnal passion of tits and finches for the seeds of flowers. It will continue just as eagerly, and will continue to enchant, until the first days of mid-winter, when tits will still be seen swinging on the frost-browned branches of the last Michaelmas daisies, plucking silver-brown darts of seeds, and an odd goldfinch or two will flash fretfully up the tall orange-tipped pagodas of the last red-hot pokers. The goldfinches, shyer now, will light up the more open spaces of the winter garden with little touches of tropical brilliance. They never come into the garden except with a kind of dancing nervousness, rarely resting, only very occasionally pausing long enough for the eye to take a quick shot of them in motionless brilliance. There was such an occasion a month ago, when they came down to the lily-pond one hot afternoon to drink and rest. A few flowers of the blush-pink water-lily were out, and as the finches rested and hovered and rested again on the flowers, which are like great sea-anemones, a small silvery grass-snake uncurled itself and swam about the green water, the pool lit up for a second or two by that strange, bright combination of flower, snake and bird.

Meanwhile the tits, with an occasional finch or two, and quite frequently sparrows, are all over the flower borders, raiding everything. Full of cheek, they are the schoolboys among birds—small Eton collars a little bedraggled, tight black caps well down over the forehead. They appear to eat anything and never rest. Their real harvest, since the Michaelmas daisies and later heleniums and sunflowers are only just past their best, has hardly begun, and there are a few seeds, too, which they will not or cannot touch : the fat turbans of hollyhocks, perhaps not yet ripe enough, the biscuit-coloured bombs of the Peruvian lilies, which crack off on hot afternoons like toy pop-guns in a silly symphony. Otherwise they raid everything, clearing up the dust and fluff of campanula and anthemis, swinging upside down on the taller salvias, quick heads very beautiful against the soft lilac bracts, having a peck at the small brown horns of Salvia patens, heads more lovely than ever against the flashing electric blue of the flowers, swinging for no apparent reason on the long-stalked Verbena bonariensis, still in full flower, with sweet buddleia-mauve heads that will not seed for a week or two. They are already scaling the full-flowered stalks of the red-hot pokers, nosing into the flower-tubes, and it is they who must have been on the acorn-hard pods of that curious plant Acanthus mollis, with its horny, pink bracts and spiky, decorative leaves for which the Greeks found so much use in architectural design. They are inexhaustible acrobats. The chaffinches and bullfinches have an almost dressed-up Sunday sedateness by contrast. Only days of cool, wet weather, when the seed is musty or sodden, seem to damp them down, and even then they are still busy selecting those seeds, like salvias, which lie deep and dry in crisp protective pockets.

There are, no doubt, choice seeds which they have missed in

the earlier summer : fat orange pills of crocus, lupins, black showers of delphinium, the crinkled charcoal scraps of the border pinks, poppies, the catapulted bullets of the hardy geranium. But they have still to enjoy the best of the year, the rich feast of berry and seed of the later autumn.

And there is no doubt that this is a vintage year for berries. Elderberries have been hanging like dark grapes. The promise of holly-berries, turning a little already from olive-green to dull crimson, is richer than for some years ; haws, which vary along one hedgerow from orange-scarlet to ripe maroon, look as luscious as cranberries. It will not be long before they are stripped bare of skin, and not long later before the first spell of frost finds bird-droppings scarlet and orange with the seed and skin of rose-hips.

Meanwhile, each evening, starlings perform a strange drama of their own. They have begun to gather on the highest branches of a group of Spanish chestnuts which have died back at their tips, so that they are like ebony skeletons against the evening sky. On these dark, naked branches the starlings descend in thousands, and the trees seem to become laden with countless gigantic seeds. Suddenly it is as if the pods of these seeds are simultaneously split open. They break from the branches with a harsh explosion, and the seeding wings lift briefly and then disperse. They blacken the air for a moment and then spread and scatter, sowing themselves into the coloured acres of sunset.